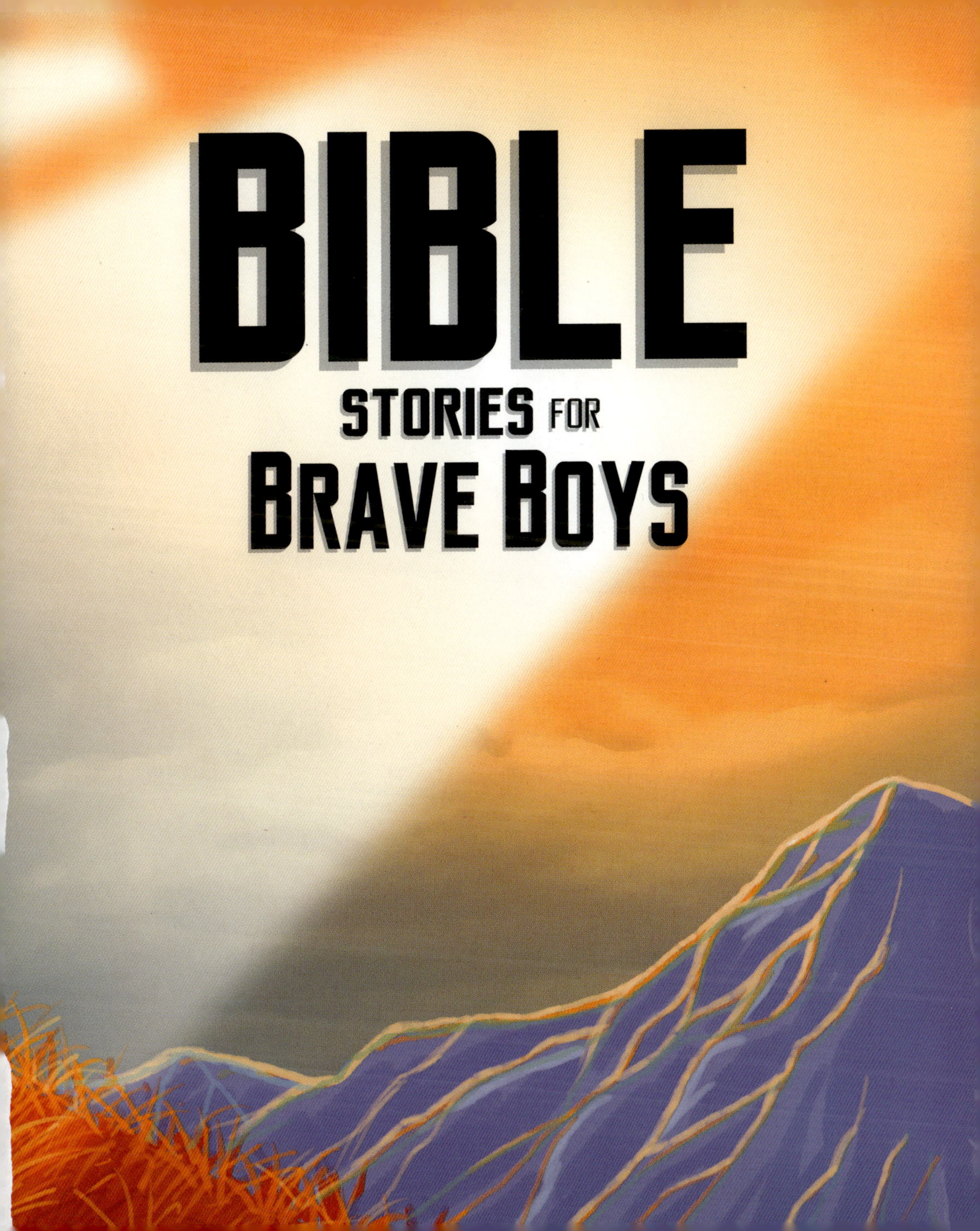

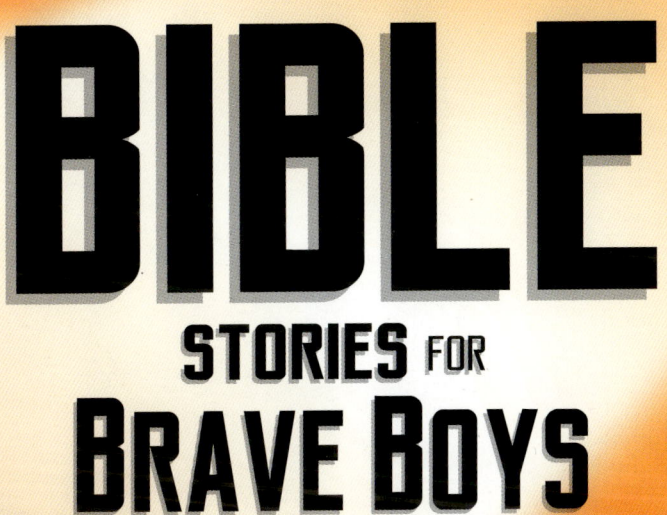

BIBLE
STORIES FOR
BRAVE BOYS

Bible Stories for Brave Boys

2nd edition, 3rd print
Copyright © Scandinavia Publishing House 2017
Drejervej 15, DK-2400 Copenhagen NV, Denmark
info@sph.as
www.sph.as

Text and illustrations copyright © Scandinavia Publishing House
Illustrations by Gustavo Mazali
Author: Melissa Alex
Editors: Alice Larsen & Vanessa Carroll
Cover design by Gao Hanyu
Book design by Isabelle Gao

Printed in China
ISBN Hardcover: 9788772030289
ISBN Softcover: 9788772030302

All rights reserved. No part of this book may be reproduced or utilized in any form or by any means, electronic or mechanical, including photocopying, recording, or by any information storage and retrieval system, without permission in writing from the publisher.

BIBLE
STORIES FOR
BRAVE BOYS

scandinavia

Contents

FOREWORD 6
THE OLD TESTAMENT 9
God Makes Heaven and Earth 11
God Makes the Creatures of the Ocean and the Sky 13
God Makes the Animals of the Earth 14

ADAM 16
Adam and Eve 19
The Garden of Eden 21
Adam and Eve Disobey God 22
Out of Eden 25
Cain and Abel 27
Cain Kills Abel 28

NOAH 30
Noah Builds an Ark 32
The Great Flood 34
Forty Days and Forty Nights of Rain 36
The Rainbow's Promise 38

ABRAHAM 40
God Chooses Abram 42
The Promise of God 45

ISAAC 46
Abraham Obeys God 48

JACOB 50
Esau Makes a Promise 52
Isaac Blesses Jacob 54

JOSEPH 56
Joseph's Dream 58
Joseph Is Thrown into a Well 60
Joseph Is Taken to Egypt 62
In the House of Potiphar 64
Joseph in Prison 66
Joseph Interprets Dreams 68
The King's Dreams 70
Joseph's Brothers Go to Egypt 72
Joseph and His Brothers Meet in Egypt 74
Joseph Tells the Truth 76

The King Welcomes Joseph's Family 78
Slavery in Egypt 80

MOSES 82
Moses Is Born 84
Saved by a Princess 86
Moses Stands Up for a Slave 88
Jethro Welcomes Moses 90
The Burning Bush 92
Ten Plagues 94
The Exodus 97
The King's Chase 98
The Parting of the Red Sea 100
The Ten Commandments 102

JOSHUA 104
Joshua Becomes the Leader of Israel 106
The Battle of Jericho 108
The Walls Come Tumbling Down 110

GIDEON 112
The Lord Chooses Gideon 114
A Small Army 116
Trumpets and Torches 118

SAMSON 120
Samson Is Born 122
Samson Fights a Lion 124
Samson and Delilah 126
Delilah Tricks Samson 129
Samson Pulls Down a Temple 130

DAVID 132
David and Saul 134
Goliath the Giant 137
David Meets Goliath 138
David Kills Goliath 140

ELIJAH 142
Elijah in the Wilderness 144
The True God 146

DANIEL 148
Daniel and His Friends 150

A Test of Faith	152
Nebuchadnezzar's Dream	154
God Reveals the Dream to Daniel	156
King Belshazzar's Banquet	158
Daniel Reads the Writing	160
Daniel in the Lions' Pit	162

THE NEW TESTAMENT 165
An Angel Visits Mary 166

JOSEPH 168
Joseph's Dream	170
Jesus Is Born	172
The Shepherds	174
The Wise Men	176
Jesus of Nazareth	178
Jesus in the Temple	180

JOHN THE BAPTIST 182
John the Baptist	184
Jesus Is Baptized	186
The Devil Tempts Jesus	188

PETER 190
Jesus Calls His First Disciples	192
Fishers of Men	194

LIFE OF JESUS
Jesus Heals a Crippled Man	196
Planting Seeds	198
True Happiness	200
Being Salt and Light	202
Do Not Worry	204
The House on the Rock	206
The Storm	208
Jesus Calms the Storm	211
Jesus Seeks a Quiet Place	213
The Hungry People	214
Five Loaves and Two Fish	216
Jesus Walks on Water	218
Peter Lacks Faith	220
Let the Children Come to Me	222
Following Jesus	224
The Good Shepherd	226
The Death of Lazarus	228
Jesus Brings Lazarus to Life	230
Who Gave the Most?	232
The Good Samaritan	234
A Rich Fool	236
The Lost Sheep and the Lost Coin	239
The Loving Father	240
Forgiven	242
God Shows Mercy	244
A Job Well Done	246
The Greatest in Heaven	248
I Am with You	251
The Rich Young Man	252
The Big Parade	254
A New Command	256
The Leaders Shall Serve	258
The Lord's Supper	260
Peter Will Deny Jesus	262
A Home in Heaven	264
The Disciples Fall Asleep	266
Betrayed with a Kiss	268
Pilate Tries to Free Jesus	270
Jesus Is Sentenced to Death	273
Jesus Is Nailed to a Cross	274
Jesus Dies	276
The Earth Trembles	278
Jesus Is Buried	280
Jesus Has Risen	282
The Empty Tomb	284
Jesus Returns to God	287

PAUL 288
Saul on the Road to Damascus	290
Paul and Silas in Jail	292
Singing in Jail	294
A Mob Turns Against Paul	296
Paul Speaks Before the Governor	298
A Stormy Voyage	300
Rome at Last	302

Foreword

Dear Reader,

We're happy to introduce you to our first Bible Stories for Brave Boys. It is our hope that this Bible story book will not only introduce you to some of the bravest people in history, but also inspire you to be a brave believer, too.

Being brave is not only about becoming someone great and important, but is just as much about sticking to the Way and continuing to believe in Jesus, even when some days are grey and make you feel indifferent. Being brave is giving thanks and rejoicing in Him, even when there seems to be no reason to do so.

In this Bible story book you'll find the accounts of many ordinary men, chosen by an extraordinary God. You will get to know the Bible characters a little better in each of their short introductions. These men trusted and obeyed God, and He gave them courage to act bravely in difficult situations. In the face of oppression, trials, and discouragements these men succeeded and ultimately changed the course of their lives, their nation, and in some cases, even the course of history. This happened not because they were superheroes, but because the God in whom they trusted gave them courage and made them brave, in spite of their fear and short comings.

God is still the same and He wants you to put your trust in Him in all situations. He will enable you to overcome trials and face challenges as well as get through the dullness of your everyday life with a brave heart and mind.

We hope and pray that this Bible Stories for Brave Boys will encourage and help you to live bravely.

We are rooting for you – and so is He!

"Since it is so likely that children will meet cruel enemies, let them at least have heard of brave knights and heroic courage. Otherwise you are making their destiny not brighter but darker."

- C.S. Lewis

The Old Testament

God Makes Heaven and Earth
Genesis 1:1-19

In the beginning, God created the heavens and the earth. The earth was a dark and empty place. There was only a roaring black ocean covering the empty form and the Spirit of God was hovering over the water. Then God said, "Let there be light!" Suddenly light shone down and He created the first day.

On the second day, God said, "Let the water above be separated from the water on the earth." The waters obeyed God's command and He called the expanse that separated the waters, sky.

On the third day, God said, "Let the waters on the earth be separated by dry land. Let there be plants and trees on the land so that the earth may be filled with living things." Land appeared to separate the oceans and trees spread their big leafy branches. Little flowers and plants sprung up out of the ground to greet the sun.

On the fourth day, God said, "Let the moon and stars shine at night, and let the sun shine by day. These lights will mark the seasons and shed light on the earth." God looked around and saw that all He had done was good.

God Makes the Creatures of the Ocean and the Sky
Genesis 1:20-23

On the fifth day, God said, "Let the ocean be filled with sea creatures!" Just then, the water began to churn with life. Great whales lifted their mighty heads. Dolphins jumped and splashed in the sunlight and little sea crabs scuttled along the sea floor. God said, "Let the sky be filled with creatures of the air!" Seagulls swooped in the breeze along with butterflies and buzzing insects. God created all of them, big and small, and He saw that it was all good.

God Makes the Animals of the Earth
Genesis 1:24-25

"Now for the dry land," God said. "Let the deserts and valleys and mountains be filled with animals!" And that's what happened. The earth was filled with wild animals to roam the land and insects to creep along the ground.

God loved watching the animals play with each other. He was very pleased with His work.

Adam

Then the Lord God formed a man from the dust of the ground and breathed into his nostrils the breath of life, and the man became a living being.
Gen 2:7

- Mentioned in: Genesis 1 Chronicles, Luke, Romans, 1 Corinthians 1 Timothy
- Meaning of name: "Man"
- Lived in: Garden of Eden, later, outside of Eden
- Married to: Eve (the first woman, "Mother of Mankind")
- Father of: Cain, Abel, Seth, other sons and daughters

Milestones:

As the first human being, Adam was by himself in the Garden of Eden for a while. Then God made Eve to be his companion and wife. Like Eve, he disobeyed God and had to bear the consequences. God knew the risk of giving people free will to choose. So He promised to send a Savior, who would bear the consequence of our disobedience and defeat death.

Questions:

Adam was alone in the Garden of Eden. He loved God, but he longed for another human being. Have you ever felt alone? Did you ask God to bring you a friend or a loved one to keep you company?

Adam and Eve
Genesis 1:26-2:3,7,18-25

On the sixth day, God looked around at all the animals of the earth and the animals of the sea and sky, and God said, "I will create human beings to rule over the animals and the land. They will be special because I will make them in My likeness."

Then, God took a handful of soil, and out of it, He made Adam. God loved Adam. He even let Adam name all the animals. But God said, "It isn't good for Adam to be alone. I will make a partner for him."

So while Adam was asleep, God took one of Adam's ribs and out of it, He created the first woman. Adam loved her and called her Eve.

God gave Adam and Eve His blessing. He said, "The earth is filled with animals you may rule over and many good plants and fruits you may eat. Fill the earth with your children, and care for all the living creatures!"

God was happy with all that He had created. It was perfect. On the seventh day, He rested from all His work.

The Garden of Eden
Genesis 2:8-17

God put Adam and Eve in a garden called Eden. The Garden of Eden was a lush and colorful paradise where they could live forever.

God placed a tree called the tree of knowledge of good and evil in the middle of the garden. God told Adam and Eve that they could eat from any of the trees in the garden except from that tree. If they ate from it, God warned, they would surely die.

Adam and Eve Disobey God
Genesis 3:1-7

One day the serpent slithered up to Eve as she was walking in the garden. "Why don't you take a bite from that juicy fruit hanging from the tree of knowledge?" he asked. Eve remembered what God had said. "God told us we must not eat fruit from that tree," she replied. To this the serpent answered with lies, "That is only because the fruit will allow you to know the difference between right and wrong. God doesn't want you to be as wise as He is."

Eve became curious. "What would be the harm in one tiny bite?" she said to herself. So she picked a fruit and tasted it. Then she handed the fruit to Adam, and he also took a bite. When they looked at each other afterwards, they realized for the first time that they were naked. They were embarrassed and quickly sewed fig leaves together to cover themselves.

Out of Eden
Genesis 3:8-19

That day, Adam and Eve heard God walking in the Garden of Eden. They were frightened because they knew they had disobeyed Him. They hid behind the trees and plants, hoping God would not discover what they had done. But God knows all things.

God called out to Adam, "Where are you?" Adam came out from hiding and told God he was afraid because he was naked. God said, "How did you know you were naked? Did you eat the fruit I told you not to eat?"

Adam answered, "Eve was the one who took the fruit. It's her fault!" And Eve said, "But it was the snake who told me to take the fruit. So it's the snake's fault!"

God loved Adam and Eve, so He was very sad that they did not obey Him, but chose to listen to the sneaky snake instead.

God gave Adam and Eve some animal skins to cover themselves. They had to leave the garden of Eden and never return, live on dry land, work hard for their food, and they would eventually die.

Cain and Abel
Genesis 4:1-5

Adam and Eve had two sons. The older son was named Cain. He farmed the land. The younger son, Abel, was a sheep farmer.

After they had been farming for some time, Cain brought some of his farm produce to God as an offering, while Abel brought the best and fattest pieces of meat from a firstborn lamb of his flock. They gave it to God by burning it on an altar they had built. God accepted Abel's offering, but He didn't accept Cain's offering because it didn't follow His instructions. For this reason, Cain was filled with jealousy toward his brother Abel.

Cain Kills Abel
Genesis 4:6-16

God said to Cain, "Why are you upset? If you do what is right, I will accept your offering! But if you do what is wrong, you are in danger. Sin is waiting to pounce on you like a lion. Don't give in to it!" But Cain wasn't listening. He was too busy trying to figure out a way he could get back at his brother.

Later, Cain went to his brother, Abel, in the field. When Cain was certain that they were all alone, he attacked his brother and killed him.

Afterward, God called out to Cain, "Where is Abel?" Cain answered, "How should I know? Am I supposed to look after my brother?" But Cain could not fool God. "Why have you done this terrible thing?" God asked him. "You've killed your own brother. From now on you will be without a home."

So Cain had to leave his family. He wandered around from place to place, never really belonging anywhere.

Noah

This is the account of Noah and his family. Noah was a righteous man, blameless among the people of his time, and he walked faithfully with God.
Gen 6:9

- Mentioned in: Genesis
- Meaning of name: "Quiet and rest"
- Lived in: Mesopotamia (modern day Iraq), before the flood, near Mount Ararat (modern day Turkey), where the ark came to rest, after the flood
- Married to: Name unknown (a woman of faith, courage, and endurance)
- Father of: Shem, Ham, Japheth

Milestones:

Noah had faith in God, which no one else did at the time. People probably thought he was crazy to build a huge boat so far from the ocean. Together with his wife, his sons and their wives, he built the ark, gathered food, endured the long voyage, and started a new life after the Great Flood.

Questions:

Standing up for God can sometimes be a difficult thing. Have you ever had to stand up for believing in God? Did anyone else stand with you?

Noah Builds an Ark
Genesis 6:5-22

The world God had made filled with more and more wicked people. God saw all their bad deeds. They cheated, stole, and lied. God was sorry He had made them, so God was sorry He had made them, so He decided to start over.

God planned a great flood. He would let rain pour down until it drenched the land and drowned the people. However, there was one man that God was pleased with. This man loved and obeyed God. His name was Noah.

God told Noah about His plan to flood the earth and put an end to all people except him and his family. God gave Noah the plans to build a giant boat called an ark.

God said, "Make it big enough to hold you and your family as well as one male and one female of every kind of animal on earth."

Noah did just as God said. He and his sons worked hard hammering wood planks together and building the ark.

After many, many years, the ark was finally finished. Noah made sure to have a special place ready for each kind of animal. He packed the ark full of food and supplies.

The Great Flood
Genesis 7:1, 10, 13-16

Noah went into the ark with his wife, his three sons, and their wives. The animals also marched inside. Two by two, the animals went into their stalls, and God closed the door to the ark. The windows of heaven were opened and the rain came pouring down – first a *pitter patter*, and then, a torrent. The dry land was covered in water and the ark began to float.

Forty Days and Forty Nights of Rain
Genesis 7:17 – 8:19

Rain poured down for forty days and forty nights. The flood was so deep that it covered the highest mountain peaks! Nothing on earth survived. Only Noah, his family, and the animals were saved. God was watching over them.

After it stopped raining, it still took many months for the water to disappear. Noah sent out a raven that flew

back and forth until the floodwaters had dried up. Noah also sent out a dove. The dove came back unable to find a place of dry land anywhere. But, when Noah sent the dove out again a week later, it returned with an olive leaf in its beak. The bird had found land!

"You can leave the ark now," God said to Noah. So Noah opened the door and called everyone out of the boat. Each of God's animals stepped off the boat, stretching their legs and sniffing the clean, fresh air. It must have felt good to walk on dry land after being penned up for so long in Noah's ark.

The Rainbow's Promise
Genesis 9:1-16

God gave a blessing to Noah and his family. He said to them, "May you have many children and grandchildren! Spread out all over the earth. It is yours. Take good care of it. I give you the plants and the animals for food. Also, I make a promise that I will keep forever: I will never again send a flood to destroy the earth."

Just then, the sun broke through the rain clouds. A beautiful rainbow full of bright colors shone in the sky.

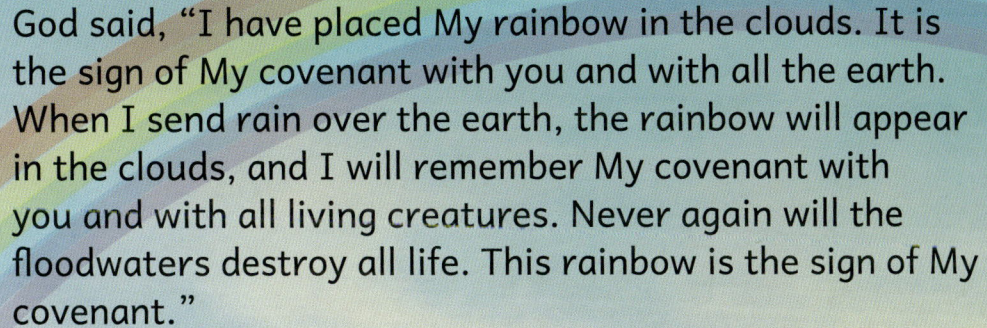

God said, "I have placed My rainbow in the clouds. It is the sign of My covenant with you and with all the earth. When I send rain over the earth, the rainbow will appear in the clouds, and I will remember My covenant with you and with all living creatures. Never again will the floodwaters destroy all life. This rainbow is the sign of My covenant."

Abraham

No longer will you be called Abram; your name will be Abraham, for I have made you a father of many nations.
Gen 17:5

- Mentioned in: Genesis, Exodus, Acts, Romans, Galatians, Hebrews
- Meaning of name: God changed his name from Abram "Exalted Father" to Abraham "Father of a Multitude"
- Lived in: Ur of the Chaldees, near Babylonia (modern day Iraq), Haran (modern day Turkey), later, Canaan (modern day Israel)
- Married to: Sarah
- Father of: Ishmael, Isaac, many others

Milestones:

Abraham left his family and land to set out on a journey to a country God had promised him. He didn't know where he was going. He just obeyed what God had told him to do. God loved him very much and called him his friend. God also promised to make him the father of many nations.

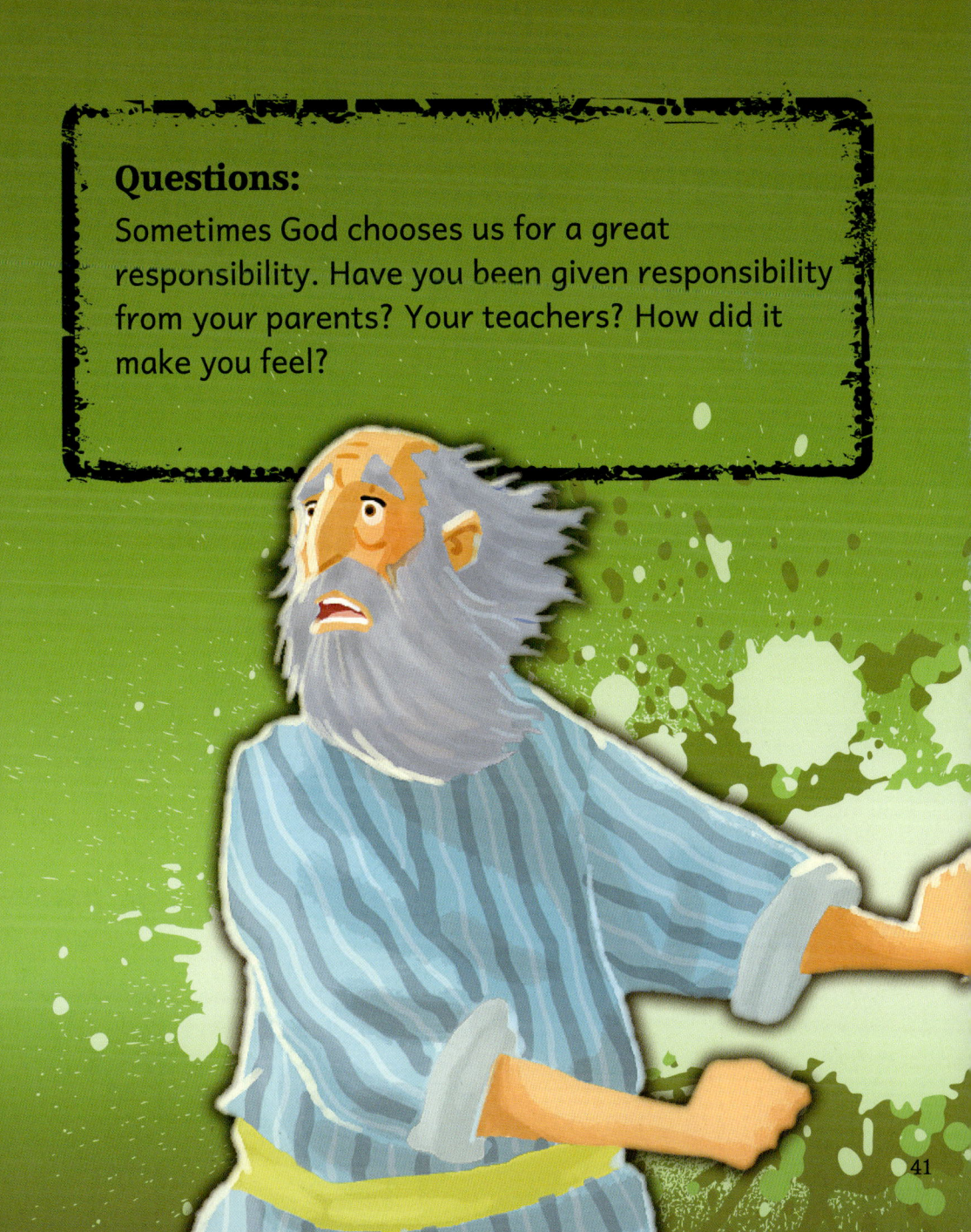

Questions:
Sometimes God chooses us for a great responsibility. Have you been given responsibility from your parents? Your teachers? How did it make you feel?

God Chooses Abram
Genesis 12:1-9

Abram was one of God's special people. He lived in the city of Haran. One day, God said to Abram, "Leave the place that you came from, and go to the land I will show you." Abram trusted God with his whole heart. He loaded his camels with all his belongings and left with his wife, Sarai, his nephew, Lot, and all their servants. They traveled through the desert hills with only God as their guide.

When Abram and his family came to the land of Canaan,

God said, "This land is yours! It will belong to your family forever. I will bless you and all the people in your family who come after you. Everyone on earth will be blessed through you!" Abram felt very thankful, so he built an altar in the desert where he could worship God. Then Abram and the rest of his group journeyed onward. Finally, they came to a place they liked and pitched their tents and settled.

The Promise of God
Genesis 17:1-19

Abram was growing older. God had given him many things—a beautiful wife, land, and animals. However, there was one thing Abram wanted that God had not given

him. Abram wanted to have a child with his wife Sarai, but God had never blessed them with one. Now they had wrinkles and gray hair. They had given up hope.

One evening, God said to Abram, "You will be the father of many nations. Look at the brilliant night sky! Can you count the stars? That is how many descendants you will have! No longer will you be called Abram. Your name will now be Abraham because you will be a father to many nations. Your wife's name will now be Sarah because you will have a son with her and kings will come from her."

Abraham said, "I trust you God! You have already given me everything I could ask for. But, can a man have a child when he is a hundred years old? Can Sarah have a child at ninety?"

God answered, "You will have a son with your wife, Sarah, and everything you have will be his." Abraham could hardly believe it. But he had faith. He got down on his knees and thanked God.

Isaac

Then God said, "Yes, but your wife Sarah will bear you a son, and you will call him Isaac. I will establish my covenant with him as an everlasting covenant for his descendants after him.
Gen 17:19

- Mentioned in: Genesis
- Meaning of name: "He laughs" Sarah laughed when God said that He would give them a child because Abraham and Sarah believed they were too old to have
- Lived in: Canaan (which is modern day Israel)
- Married to: Rebekah
- Father of: Esau, Jacob

Milestones:

Isaac lived a life devoted to God. He remembered that God provided another sacrifice and saved his life. He also only took one wife during a time when men would often take more than one. He loved his wife, Rebekah, very much.

Questions:

We should always remember God's hand in our life, just as Isaac remembered how God saved him. What do you have in your life that you can thank God for?

Abraham Obeys God
Genesis 21:1-7; 22:6-18

God gave Abraham and Sarah a son and they called him Isaac. After several years had passed, God decided to test Abraham's trust and obedience. God said to Abraham, "Go get Isaac, your son, whom you love so dearly. Take him to the high mountaintop of Moriah and sacrifice him on an alter in honor of Me." Abraham's heart nearly broke with sadness when he heard God's words. Isaac was the child God had given him, and now God was asking him to sacrifice his beloved child! But Abraham was filled with faith and love for God. He knew that his only choice was to obey.

Abraham got up early the next morning and chopped wood for the altar. He tied the wood into bundles. Then he told Isaac to come with him up the steep mountain. Abraham and Isaac were out of breath by the time they reached the top. Abraham took the wood and coals and made an altar in the spot where God had told him to sacrifice Isaac. Then Isaac said, "Father, we have the coals and the wood, but where is the lamb for the sacrifice?" Abraham answered sadly, "God will provide the lamb, son."

Abraham tied up Isaac and placed him on the altar. Just as he was about to kill him, the voice of God called out,

"Stop, Abraham! Don't kill Isaac! Now I know that you are willing to sacrifice what is most precious to you. You trusted Me and obeyed My command. Therefore, I will bless your family forever."

Abraham sighed with relief. He looked up and saw a ram caught by its horns in the bushes. He took the ram and sacrificed it in place of his son. Then Abraham and Isaac went home with happy hearts, grateful to God.

Jacob

Then the man said, "Your name will no longer be Jacob, but Israel, because you have struggled with God and with humans and have overcome."
Gen 32:28

- Mentioned in: Genesis
- Meaning of name: "Grasps at heels" (Jacob held onto his twin brother Esau's heel when he was born) -- God renamed him Israel, meaning "He struggles with God" after he wrestled with God
- Lived in: Canaan (modern day Israel), stayed with uncle in Haran (modern day Turkey) for 20 years, back to Canaan, later Egypt
- Married to: Leah, Rachel
- Father of: Reuben, Simeon, Levi, Judah, Dan, Naphtali, Gad, Asher, Issachar, Zebulun, Dinah, Joseph and Benjamin

Milestones:

As the father of the heads of the Twelve Tribes of Israel, including Joseph, who would become a powerful figure in Egypt, Jacob passed on the faith of his father, Isaac, and his grandfather, Abraham, to his family.

Questions:

Jacob was a hardworking, dedicated man. He worked fourteen years in order to marry the woman he loved. Have you ever had to work for something you wanted? Did you come to learn that hard work brings fruitful results?

Esau Makes a Promise
Genesis 25:27-34

When Isaac grew up and married, he became the father of twin sons, Esau and Jacob. Esau became an excellent hunter, while Jacob tended sheep. Esau was his father's favorite son, but Jacob was his mother's favorite son. Because Esau was the oldest, he had certain birthrights that Jacob did not have.

One evening, Jacob was cooking a stew at his camp. Esau came back from a hunt and smelled the delicious food wafting up from the pot. "That red stew you're cooking smells good, brother. May I have some?" Esau asked.

"Yes," Jacob said, "I will give you some of my stew if you promise to give me something in return." "What do you want?" asked Esau, who was growing hungrier by the minute and was happy to agree to anything. "Your birthright," replied Jacob. Esau quickly reached for the bowl of stew. "Sure, why not?" Esau said without a thought. "What good is t to me if I die from hunger?" Then he gulped down the stew while Jacob smiled to himself. Jacob knew that he had tricked his brother.

Isaac Blesses Jacob
Genesis 27:1-40

Isaac was now old and blind and knew he was close to dying. Before he died, he wanted to give his oldest son, Esau, a special blessing. It was part of his birthright as the eldest son. Because Rebekah loved Jacob best, she wanted him to have the blessing instead of his brother.

"Go to your father," Rebekah said to Jacob, after Esau left to go hunting. "He will think you are your brother, Esau, and he will give you his blessing!" Jacob said, "My brother is a hairy man, and I am not. If my father finds out I am tricking him, I will bring down a curse on my head!" Rebekah was a clever woman. She quickly took some goatskins and wrapped them around Jacob's arms.

Jacob then went to his father and said, "It's me, Esau." Isaac reached out and felt his hairy arms, and believed that he was telling the truth. He laid his hands on his son's head and gave a blessing that made Jacob lord over all his family, including Esau.

When Esau came home, he rushed to see his father. "Father, it's Esau—I'm home from my hunt, and I've brought you some meat!" Isaac suddenly realized he had given his blessing to the wrong son! Esau became furious and his father was upset, but it was already too late. Jacob had received the blessing.

Joseph

Then Joseph said to his brothers, "Come close to me." When they had done so, he said, "I am your brother Joseph, the one you sold into Egypt! And now, do not be distressed and do not be angry with yourselves for selling me here, because it was to save lives that God sent me ahead of you."
Gen 45:4-5

- Mentioned in: Genesis
- Meaning of name: "To increase"
- Lived in: Haran (modern day Turkey), Canaan (modern day Israel), Egypt
- Married to: Asenat (daughter of an Egyptian priest at Ra's temple)
- Father of: Ephraim, Manasseh

Milestones:

God gave Joseph a gift of wisdom and interpreting dreams. This gift saved not only his own life, but the life of his family and people. Because of his goodness, faith in God, and talents, he rose in ranks until he became a very powerful figure in Egypt, able to provide for the whole nation.

Questions:

Joseph's brothers betrayed him, but because he was a Godly man, he forgave them. Has someone ever hurt you? Did they come to you and ask for forgiveness? Did you forgive them?

Joseph's Dream
Genesis 37:1-11

Jacob married and had many sons, but his favorite son was Joseph. When Joseph was a teenager, he helped his older brothers take care of the sheep. One day, Jacob gave Joseph a gift. It was a coat so colorful and bright that it was impossible not to stare at Joseph when he wore it. His brothers were jealous. They knew their father loved Joseph more than he loved them. One evening, Joseph had a dream. He told his brothers about it. "We were tying up bundles of wheat in a field. My bundle stood up, and your bundles bowed down to it."

His brothers scoffed, "So you think you'll rule over us, do you?" Joseph had another dream. He told his brothers, but they just laughed and made fun of him again. So Joseph

went to tell his father. "The sun and the moon and eleven stars bowed down to me," he explained. "What can it mean?" his father asked. "Will your mother and I and your brothers one day bow down to you?" Joseph didn't know. However, Jacob kept thinking about his son's dream.

Joseph Is Thrown into a Well
Genesis 37:12-24

One day, Joseph's brothers had taken their sheep to graze in a pasture near Shechem. Jacob told Joseph, "Go and find out how your brothers are doing." So Joseph searched and found his brothers in a place called Dothan. When Joseph's brothers saw him coming, they pointed and laughed. "Look," they said, "it's the dreamer! Why don't we throw him into a pit full of wild animals, then we'll see what happens to those dreams." Reuben was Joseph's older brother and felt responsible for him. "Let's not kill him," he said. "Let's just throw him into a dry well." Secretly, Reuben planned to go back and rescue Joseph after his brothers left. As soon as Joseph walked up to them, they tackled him to the ground and tore off his colorful coat. Then, they threw him into a dry well so deep that he could not get out.

Joseph Is Taken to Egypt
Genesis 37:25-35

Joseph's brothers went back to their camp to eat. They heard a caravan walking by and looked up. It was a group of Ishmaelites heading toward Egypt. Their camels were loaded with spices and perfumes that they were going to sell in the marketplace.

Judah, another one of Joseph's brothers, said, "What will we get out of throwing Joseph in a well? If we can sell him to these traders, we'll make some money. After all, Joseph is our brother." So the brothers ran back and pulled Joseph up out of the well. They sold him to the Ishmaelites for twenty pieces of silver. As they watched

the caravan rattle away down the track, "What are we going to say to our father?" they asked each other. So they came up with a plan. First, they killed a goat. Then, they dipped Joseph's coat in the goat's blood. When they came home, they held up Joseph's coat and showed their father. "Isn't this Joseph's coat?" they asked him. "Yes," Jacob cried out, "he must have been torn to pieces by some wild animal!" Then he hid his face in his hands and cried. The brothers tried to comfort him, but it was of no use. He told them, "I will be sad until the day I die."

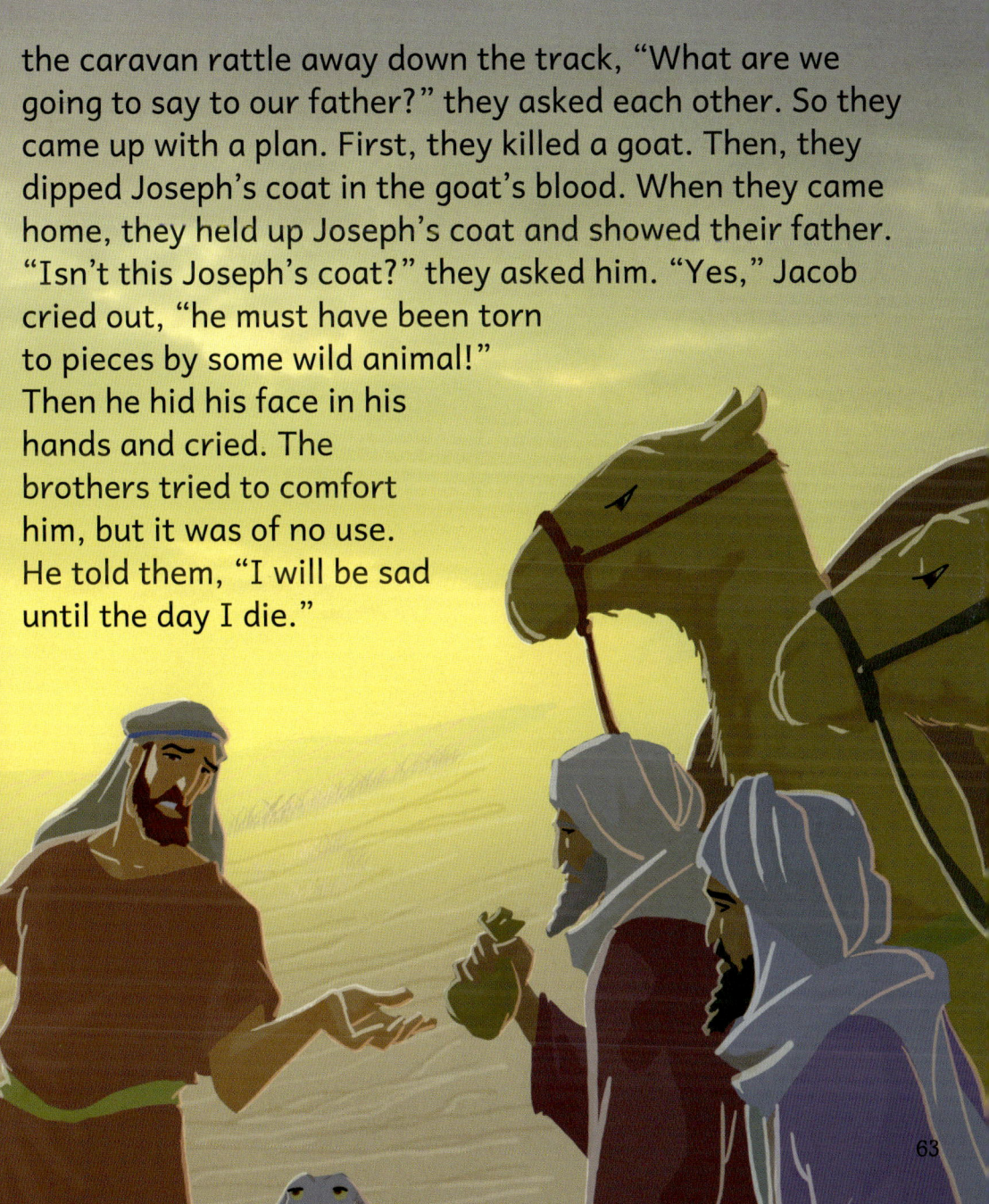

In the House of Potiphar
Genesis 39:1-6

Meanwhile, Joseph had arrived in Egypt. The Ishmaelite traders sold him to a man named Potiphar who was one of the king's most important officials. He kept Joseph in his house as a servant. While Joseph did his work, Potiphar watched him very closely. There was something special about Joseph. It was as if everything he did turned out to be a success. That was because the Lord was with Joseph.

So Potiphar made Joseph his personal assistant. He put Joseph in charge of his house and all of his property. Because of Joseph, Potiphar didn't worry about a single thing in his house, except for the food he ate. And because of Joseph, God blessed Potiphar's house and all he owned.

Joseph in Prison
Genesis 39:7-20

Joseph was not only smart; he was also strong and handsome. After a while, Potiphar's wife began to take an interest in him. "Come, sleep with me," she said to him one day. Joseph told her, "Potiphar has put me in charge of everything he owns. The one thing he hasn't given me is you. So why would I want to sin against God and take you from him?" Then he turned around and left. But Potiphar's wife didn't give up. She kept begging him to be with her. Joseph tried to ignore her, but one day, she found him alone in a room. She caught him by his coat, but Joseph wriggled out of it and left the room.

Potiphar's wife yelled, "Help! Help! I've just been attacked!" The servants came running in, and she held up Joseph's coat. "Look," she cried, "Joseph has just attacked me. Here's his coat to prove it!" When Potiphar came home, his wife told him the same lie she had told the servants. He was outraged and threw Joseph in prison, where all the criminals were kept.

Joseph Interprets Dreams
Genesis 40:1-23

Sometime later, the king's cook as well as his personal servant had made the king angry. He threw them into the same prison where Joseph was locked up. One night, while they were sleeping in their cell, the servant and the cook had strange dreams. They woke up puzzled. They wondered what the dreams meant. "God knows the meaning of your dreams," Joseph told them. "Tell me your dreams, and I will tell you what they mean." So the servant told him, "I saw three branches ripe with grapes. I squeezed the juice from them and served it to the king." "In three days you will be forgiven," Joseph told him. "You'll serve the king just like you used to do. When these things happen, tell the king about me, and help me get out of here."

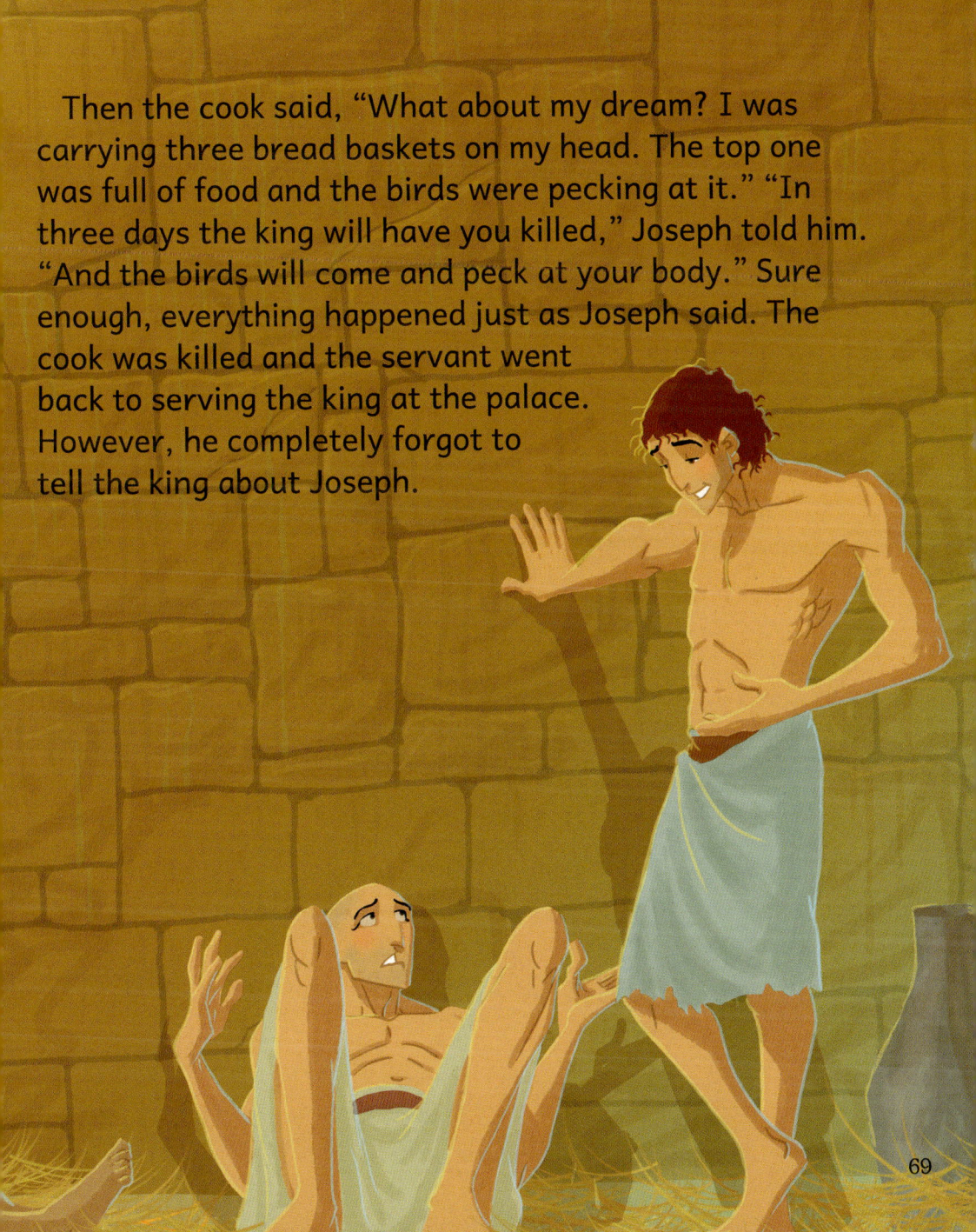

Then the cook said, "What about my dream? I was carrying three bread baskets on my head. The top one was full of food and the birds were pecking at it." "In three days the king will have you killed," Joseph told him. "And the birds will come and peck at your body." Sure enough, everything happened just as Joseph said. The cook was killed and the servant went back to serving the king at the palace. However, he completely forgot to tell the king about Joseph.

The King's Dreams
Genesis 41:1-32

Two years later, the king of Egypt had two separate dreams that frightened him. He called in his magicians, but they did not know what the dreams meant. So he called in his wise men, but they did not know either. That's when the servant remembered Joseph. "Your Majesty," he said, "when I was in prison, there was a young Hebrew who could tell the meaning of dreams. Everything he said came true." The king was willing to try anything, so he sent for Joseph. Joseph shaved and changed his clothes, then he went in to see the king. The king told him, "I was standing on the banks of the Nile River in my dream. I watched as seven fat and healthy cows came out of the water. Then seven sick cows came out of the water, too and

ate the healthy ones. I also dreamed that seven full heads of grain were swallowed up by seven dry heads of grain."
"This is what your dreams mean," Joseph told the king. "There will be seven years of plenty. You and your people will have everything that you need, but then there will be a famine. For seven years Egypt will not have enough to eat. People everywhere will go hungry."

Joseph's Brothers Go to Egypt
Genesis 42:1-7

Joseph advised the king to store up grain from the seven good years, so the Egyptians would not need to starve during the seven bad years. The king then made Joseph governor and head of that project. In this way, he became the most important man after the king.

When the bad years came, Joseph's father and brothers in Canaan were also starving. Jacob told his sons, "Go to Egypt and buy some grain for us." So the ten brothers left

for Egypt but Jacob didn't let his youngest son, Benjamin, go. He loved Benjamin just like he used to love Joseph. He was afraid of letting Benjamin go anywhere, so he always kept him at home.

The brothers traveled across the desert and into Egypt. They went to the governor and bowed before him. They didn't realize that the governor was their very own brother.

Joseph and His Brothers Meet in Egypt
Genesis 42:8-24

Joseph recognized them right away but didn't tell them. "You are spies!" he told them angrily. "No, we're not!" they replied. "We are twelve brothers, but one is dead, and the youngest is at home with our father."

"Let's see if you're telling the truth," Joseph said. "All but one of you go home and get your youngest brother. Bring him back to me. If you don't, I will put you to death."

The brothers whispered to one another in their own language, "We are being punished by God because we were cruel to Joseph. God saw how we paid no attention to his cries and sold him like an animal long ago."

Joseph understood what they were saying, and he turned away so they couldn't see him and cried.

So the brothers went back to Canaan and convinced their father that Benjamin had to come with them.

Joseph Tells the Truth
Genesis 45:1-15

When Joseph saw Benjamin, he knew it was time to tell his brothers the truth. "Come up close to me," he told them. His brothers obeyed, but they didn't understand why he had tears in his eyes. Then he spoke, "I'm your brother Joseph! You sold me long ago to the Ishmaelites. Don't blame yourselves for what you did," Joseph continued. "Even though you were cruel to me, it worked out in a wonderful way. The Lord let me save you and many other

people from going hungry. Go home and tell your father his son is alive and that God has made me a ruler of Egypt!"

Joseph's brothers could not believe it. Their faces lit up with joy. They were grateful their brother forgave them. Joseph went over to Benjamin. They cried and kissed each other. Then Joseph hugged and kissed each one of his other brothers. He again urged his brothers to go back home and tell his father that his son Joseph was alive. "And bring him back here to live with me," Joseph said.

The King Welcomes Joseph's Family
Genesis 45:16-28

When the king heard that Joseph's brothers had come to Egypt, he was pleased and told Joseph, "Have your brothers return to Canaan and give them some extra wagons for their wives and children to ride back in. Be sure they bring your father. Tell him he does not have to bring anything. I will make sure he gets all the best things in Egypt."

Slavery in Egypt
Exodus 1:6-22

Joseph's family lived in the region of Goshen for four hundred years. They grew in number and were called Hebrews. While Joseph was alive, they lived in peace. But many years after Joseph had died, a new king ruled over Egypt. This king did not know about all the good things Joseph had done. He wanted the Hebrews out of Egypt. "They have taken over our land," he complained. "Soon they will take over our people, too." The king forced the Hebrews to be slaves. They had to work all day whether it was roasting hot or freezing cold. They had to mix cement and carry bricks and build entire cities. It was hard work, and they were treated very harshly. But even though the

work was miserable, their families grew larger and spread throughout the land. This just made the Egyptians hate them even more. The king called in two Hebrew midwives, Shiprah and Puah, to see him. He told them, "I want you to kill every baby boy among the Hebrews." The midwives feared God more than they feared the king, so they did not obey his command.

When the king found out, he became very angry. "Didn't you hear me?" he said. "I told you to kill all the Hebrew boys as they are born!" The women made up a story. "Your majesty," they told him. "Hebrew women have their babies much quicker than Egyptian women, they give birth before we arrive." So the king sent out a command all over Egypt saying, "As soon as a Hebrew boy is born, he must be thrown into the Nile River!"

Moses

Then Moses stretched out his hand over the sea, and all that night the Lord drove the sea back with a strong east wind and turned it into dry land. The waters were divided, and the Israelites went through the sea on dry ground, with a wall of water on their right and on their left.
Ex 14:21-22

- Mentioned in: Exodus, Leviticus, Numbers, Deuteronomy
- Meaning of name: "Drawn out of water"
- Lived in: Egypt, fled to Midian (because he had killed an Egyptian) – God later sent Moses back to Egypt to lead His people from slavery to the Promised Land
- Married to: Zipporah
- Father of: Gershom, Eliezer
- Related to: Aaron (his brother), Miriam (his sister)

Milestones:

Moses led his people, the Israelites, out of Egypt and to the edge of the Promised Land. Though growing up as a prince in Egypt, he gave up that life when he fled from Egypt, God used him to save His people from the Egyptians' cruelty.

Questions:

Moses spoke face to face with God, one of the only people to ever "see" God. How do you speak with God? How can we communicate with Him and how does He speak to us?

Moses Is Born
Exodus 2:1-4

While the Israelites were slaves to the Egyptians, the king issued a command to kill all sons born to Israelites so they wouldn't take over his country. During this time, there was a man and a woman, from the Hebrew tribe of Levi, living in Egypt. The woman had just given birth to a baby boy. When she heard the king's order, she panicked. She loved her baby; he was her pride and joy. So, she searched her house and found a spot where she could hide him.

She was able to keep him hidden for three months. The king's officials were roaming the country and were killing every baby boy that belonged to the Hebrews. The woman decided she had to find a better hiding spot. First, she took a basket made of papyrus reeds and made it waterproof with tar. Next, she put her baby in the basket. Then, she sneaked down to the riverbank, and let the basket float among the bulrushes on the water. Miriam, the baby's older sister, had followed her mother down to the river. Her mother went back home, but Miriam stayed crouching down in the grass. She wanted to watch over her brother and see what would happen to him.

Saved by a Princess
Exodus 2:5-10

While Miriam was watching her brother, the king's daughter came down to the river to bathe. As she approached the riverbank, she saw something floating on the water. She told her servant to wade into the river and fetch whatever was floating in it. They were surprised to find a basket with a little baby boy inside.

The princess immediately picked up the baby and rocked

him gently. Miriam hurried over and said, "Princess, I see that you love this little baby. Perhaps I can find a woman to care for him until he is old enough for you to keep."

The princess smiled at Miriam. "Yes, that's a fine idea," she said. So Miriam took her little brother back to their mother to nurse him until he was old enough to be adopted. She then took him to the princess, who named him Moses.

Moses Stands Up for a Slave
Exodus 2:11-15

Moses grew up in the palace. He was treated like a prince and had the best of everything, plenty to eat, and the finest clothes. One day, Moses took a walk outside of the palace grounds. He saw the Hebrews, his people, slaving away under the hot sun. Then, he noticed that one of them was being beaten by an Egyptian slave master. Moses was furious and ran over to save the man who was being beaten. He grabbed the slave master with both hands and killed him. Moses hid the body in the sand. But someone found out about what he had done. Everyone began to gossip about Moses. The king heard and was so angry that he sent his men to arrest Moses and have him killed. Moses had to run away. He did not stop until he crossed the border and reached the land of Midian in the desert.

Jethro Welcomes Moses
Exodus 2:14-21

Once Moses arrived in Midian, he sat down by a well and had a drink of water. Just then, the seven daughters of a priest named Jethro came to the well to give water to their sheep and goats. However, a group of shepherds tried to bully them. Moses stood up for the girls and chased the shepherds away. Then, Moses offered to water the women's sheep and goats himself. They thanked him and went back to their father's house.

"Why do you come so early today?" their father asked when they came in. The women told him about the shepherds who bullied them. "But

a young Hebrew helped us," they explained. "and he even watered our flocks."

"Why didn't you invite him to our home?" Jethro replied. "We must return his kindness and let him stay with us."

The girls went back to find Moses. They invited him to come and live with them. So Moses stayed with Jethro, and eventually married one of his daughters, named Zipporah.

The Burning Bush
Exodus 3:1-10

One day, Moses was guarding Jethro's sheep and goats on the mountainside. He was wandering along the trail when, suddenly, something incredible happened. He saw a bush light up in flames. As he stepped closer to get a better look, he noticed that the bush was not burning up. Suddenly, the voice of God called to Moses from the bush, "Moses! Don't come any closer. Take your shoes off, for this is holy ground. I am the God of Abraham, Isaac, and Jacob." Then, Moses covered his face for he was afraid to see God.

"Moses, I am here to tell you that I have not forgotten My beloved people. I know that they are suffering as slaves in Egypt. I have heard their cries and I will answer their prayers. I have something special in store for them. I have chosen you, Moses, to lead My people out of Egypt. You will bring them safely to the land I have promised your ancestors."

Ten Plagues
Exodus 7:14–11:10; 12:29-32

Moses and his brother Aaron went to see the king of Egypt. The king, Pharaoh, did not want to let the Hebrew people go. Because Pharaoh did not obey, God inflicted plagues upon Pharaoh and Egypt.

First, God turned the Nile River into blood. But Pharaoh did not let the Israelites go. So God brought thousands of frogs to Egypt. But still Pharaoh refused God's order. God brought gnats, flies, and allowed Egypt's livestock to die from disease. Still Pharaoh refused. God brought

boils and a thunderstorm of hail and locusts that ate everything growing in the fields, but still Pharaoh's heart was hardened. Pharaoh said "No." So God darkened the sky, even during the day, and still, Pharaoh was stubborn.

So God told Moses that He would bring a final, tenth plague upon Egypt: "I will strike down the firstborn of both people and cattle," God said. However, God promised not to kill the Israelites' first born if they painted lamb's blood above their doors. So it happened that all the first born were struck down except the Israelites. Pharaoh finally recognized God's power and told Moses to leave with His people.

The Exodus
Exodus 13:17-14:4

God led His people through the deserts of Egypt. He never left them. During the day, He appeared as a cloud leading the way before them. At night, He lit up their path in the form of a pillar of fire. The people walked a long way, and when they came to a place called Etham near the border, they needed a rest. They set up camp and spent the night there. The next day, God told them to camp in a different spot. He knew the king and his army would chase after Israel. He was going to show His great power and help the Israelites win. The people obeyed and camped where God led them. Then they pitched their tents, tied up their animals, and went to sleep.

The King's Chase
Exodus 14:5-14

The king of Egypt was told that the Hebrews had fled. "Look what we've done!" he shouted to his men. "We let them go, and now we'll have no slaves." Six hundred horse-drawn chariots were loaded with soldiers. The king led them on a chase to capture the Israelite people.

When the Israelites saw the chariots heading toward them from afar, they were frightened and ran to Moses. "You brought us out of slavery only to die here in the desert," they moaned, "and now the king will kill us all!" But Moses knew that the Lord had a plan. "Don't be afraid," he said. "You will see God work His miracles. Have faith! God will take care of us."

The Parting of the Red Sea
Exodus 14:15-31

God told Moses, "Tell the people to start heading toward the Red Sea. When you get to the water, raise your staff and stretch out your hand. I will part the waters, and you will be able to march across to the other side." So Moses led the people toward the sea. As they approached the shore, Moses held his hand out. All night, a strong east wind drove the sea back and turned it into dry land. Now Israel could cross the Red Sea. The Egyptian army was amazed. They followed right behind in their chariots.

Once Moses reached the other side, he waited until all the people had safely crossed over. Then he held his hand above the water, and the waves crashed together again. The Egyptian army drowned with their chariots in the wild, foamy waves. When the Israelites saw how God saved them, they respected God and put their faith in Him and His servant Moses.

The Ten Commandments
Exodus 19:16-20:17, 24:12

When the Israelites reached Mount Sinai, they camped there for some time. God told Moses to climb the mountain and meet Him there. Moses reached the top, and God spoke to him from the blazing fire. "I am God, the One who has brought you out of slavery in Egypt," He said. "These are My Ten Commandments:

Do not worship any God but Me.
Do not worship idols and false images.
Do not swear and misuse My name.
Remember the seventh day—the Sabbath, and keep it holy.

Respect your father and mother.
Do not murder.
Be faithful in marriage.
Do not steal.
Do not tell lies about others.
Do not want anything that belongs to someone else."

When God had finished speaking to Moses, He gave him two stone tablets with the Ten Commandments carved into them.

Joshua

Then Moses summoned Joshua and said to him in the presence of all Israel, "Be strong and courageous, for you must go with this people into the land that the Lord swore to their ancestors to give them, and you must divide it among them as their inheritance. The Lord himself goes before you and will be with you; he will never leave you nor forsake you. Do not be afraid; do not be discouraged."
Deut 31:7-8

- Mentioned in: Exodus, Numbers, Deuteronomy, Joshua, Judges, 1 Samuel, 1 Chronicles, Nehemiah, Acts, Hebrews
- Meaning of name: "The Lord is salvation" –similar in meaning to Jesus' ("He will save")
- Lived in: Egypt, the wilderness, and the "Promised Land"
- Married to: Unknown
- Father of: Unknown

Milestones:

Joshua led the Israelites into the Promised Land after the death of Moses. Joshua was a faithful leader, always turning to God for advice, even when others were telling him to do differently.

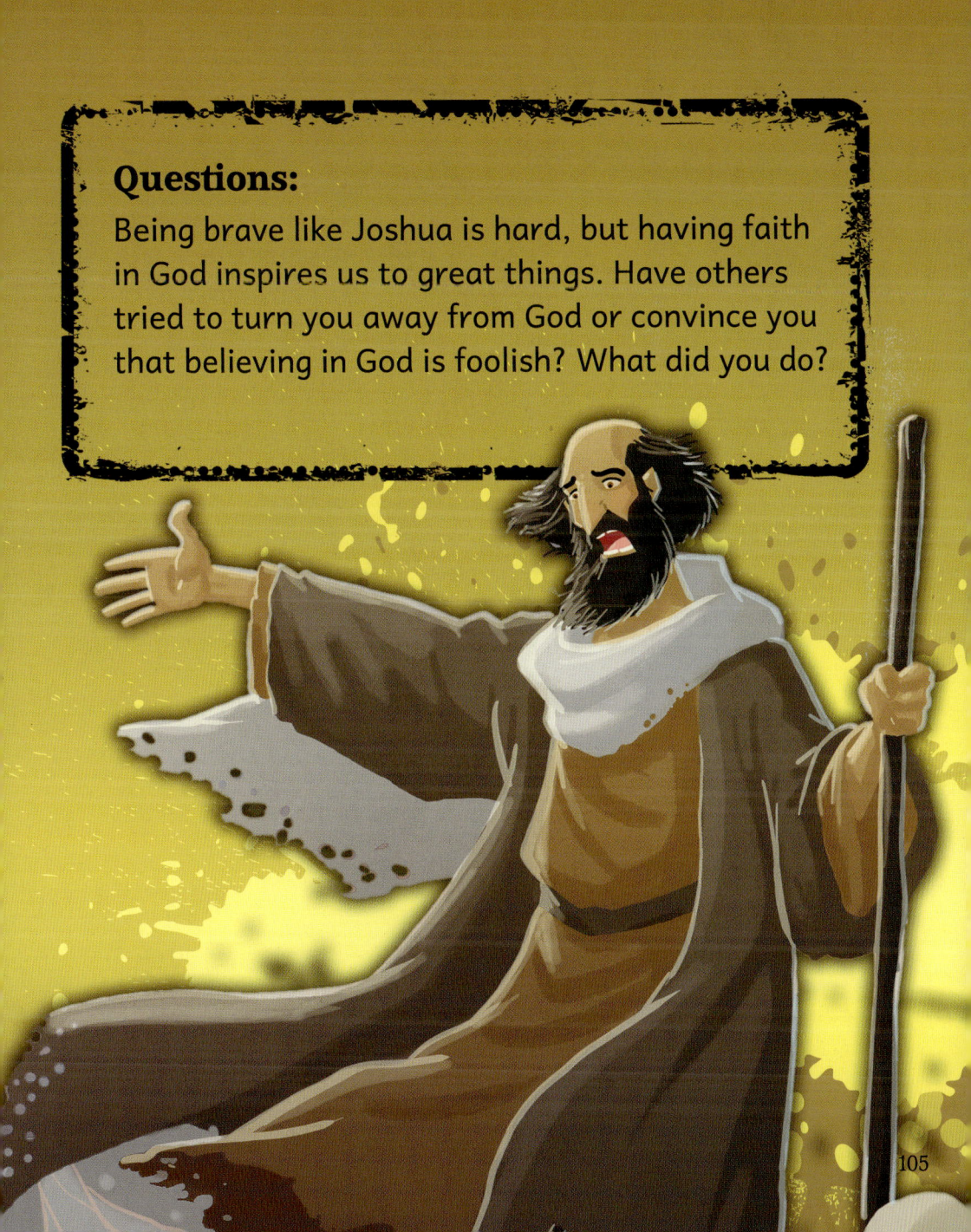

Questions:

Being brave like Joshua is hard, but having faith in God inspires us to great things. Have others tried to turn you away from God or convince you that believing in God is foolish? What did you do?

Joshua Becomes the Leader of Israel
Joshua 1:1-9

When the Israelites finally reached the border of the Promised Land, Moses died. Aaron and Miriam had also died. Who would lead the Israelites into the land? Then God spoke to Joshua, who had been Moses' special helper, "Now that Moses is gone, you must lead the people across the Jordan River into the Promised Land. Wherever you go, I will give you that land. I will be with you, just as I was with Moses. Be strong and brave. Remember what Moses taught you. Read the Book of Law and obey my words. Do not be afraid or discouraged. The Lord your God will be with you wherever you go." So Joshua became the new leader of Israel.

The Battle of Jericho
Joshua 6:1-14

Jericho was a city with a high wall around it to protect the people of Jericho from their enemies. God told Joshua he was giving Jericho to the Israelites. The people of Jericho knew that the Israelites were coming. They stayed in their houses, shut the windows, and locked the doors. All the while, Israel marched closer to Jericho. God told Joshua what to do. "March quietly around the city one time every day," He said. "Do this for six days. Carry the Ark of the Covenant, the sacred chest, in front of you, and have the priests hold trumpets. Then, on the seventh day, march

seven times around the city. Then blow the trumpets and shout! I will let you defeat the king of Jericho and his entire army. All the walls will fall down, and you can run into the city from every side." Joshua listened carefully to God's plan. When they finally reached Jericho, Joshua told the people what God had said. The people agreed, so Joshua shouted, "Let's march!" The priests went in front carrying the Ark of the Covenant. Some of them held trumpets. Then the people marched behind them. The walls of Jericho towered above them, but the people trusted the Lord's plan. They marched around quietly, once a day, for six days.

The Walls Come Tumbling Down
Joshua 6:15-27

On the seventh day, the people of Israel woke up early. They began to march around Jericho. One, two, three, four, five, six times they marched around the town. On the seventh time, Joshua called out, "Get ready to shout! Let your voices carry up to God. He will give you Jericho!" The people circled around one last time. This time the priests blasted their trumpets and the people shouted. The walls crumbled and fell down, then people ran into Jericho from every side. The Lord let Israel conquer Jericho that day.

Gideon

The three companies blew the trumpets and smashed the jars. Grasping the torches in their left hands and holding in their right hands the trumpets they were to blow, they shouted, "A sword for the Lord and for Gideon!" While each man held his position around the camp, all the Midianites ran, crying out as they fled.
Judges 7: 20-21

- Mentioned in: Judges
- Meaning of name: "One who cuts down"
- Lived in: Manasseh (modern day Israel)
- Married to: many wives
- Father of: seventy sons, Jeter (the firstborn), Jotam (the lastborn), Abimelech (his mother was not Gideon's wife)

Milestones:

Gideon's faith came slowly, but once he believed, he never let God down. He was a faithful warrior and leader to the Israelites against worshipers of Baal and other enemies.

Questions:
Gideon became strong because of his faith in God. In what way do you think your faith can make you feel strong?

The Lord Chooses Gideon
Judges 6:11-24

After the Israelites had settled in the Promised Land, they started to worship other gods. So the Lord let the neighboring nations attack and plunder them. When the Israelites had had enough, they cried to God for help, and He would raise up someone to help save them from their enemies.

When the Midianites had ruled Israel for seven years,

the Lord sent an angel to the town of Ophrah. The angel sat down under a big oak tree. A young man, named Gideon, was threshing wheat in a winepress nearby. The angel said, "The Lord is with you. You are a strong warrior." Gideon replied, "Then why are these awful things happening to us? We hear the stories of how God rescued our ancestors in Egypt. But I think He must have forgotten about us. He hasn't done anything to save us from the Midianites." This time, the Lord spoke, "Go in the strength you have. I am choosing you to save Israel." "Why choose me?" Gideon asked. "My clan is the weakest among our tribe and I am no one special." The Lord answered, "You can rescue Israel because I am going to be with you." "Give me a sign that you are really the Lord," Gideon said. "Wait here, and I will prepare an offering." So Gideon killed a young goat and boiled the meat. He placed the meat and some bread on a rock by the angel of the Lord. Then Gideon watched as the angel touched the offering with the tip of his staff. The offering caught fire and the smoke rose up to the sky and the angel disappeared. Gideon built an altar to God. He called the altar, "The Lord is peace."

A Small Army
Judges 7:1-8

After he had called the other Israelite tribes to go to war, Gideon and his army traveled to a spring called Harod. They camped there for the night. The Lord told Gideon, "Your army is too big. If you win with a big army, the people will think they have done this great thing instead of Me. Let everyone who is afraid go home." So thousands of men got up and turned around to go home. There were still ten thousand men left. The Lord told Gideon, "You need

a smaller army. Take the men down to the spring, and I will test them. Some of them will go with you, and some will go home." So Gideon led his army down to the spring. The Lord said to Gideon, "Watch how the men get a drink of water. Divide the men into two groups: those who cup their hands and lap up water like a dog and those who kneel to drink." Three hundred men lapped up the water, and the rest kneeled. The Lord said, "Take all the men who lapped up water like a dog. The rest can go home." Gideon was left with an army of only three hundred men.

Trumpets and Torches
Judges 7:16-24, 8:29

Gideon divided his men into three groups and handed out a trumpet to each of his soldiers. Then he handed out clay jars with a torch inside. He told them, "We attack from three sides. Carry your trumpets. When you hear my signal, blow them as loud as you can. Then smash the clay jars and hold your torches up high. Now, let's go fight for the Lord!" In the middle of the night, Gideon and his army sneaked up to the enemy camp. They took their positions. When Gideon blew his trumpet signal, all the soldiers picked up their trumpets and blew as loud as they could. Then they shouted, "Fight with your swords for the

Lord and for Gideon!" They smashed their clay jars and held up the burning torches. The Midianites heard the mighty sound and ran, crying out as they fled. They picked up their swords, but the Lord made them confused. They began to fight their own people. Some of them tried to run away and cross the Jordan River, but Gideon already had every spring, stream, and river guarded. Not one single enemy could escape.

Samson

Then Samson prayed to the Lord, "Sovereign Lord, remember me. Please, God, strengthen me just once more, and let me with one blow get revenge on the Philistines for my two eyes." Then Samson reached toward the two central pillars on which the temple stood. Bracing himself against them, his right hand on the one and his left hand on the other, Samson said, "Let me die with the Philistines!" Then he pushed with all his might, and down came the temple on the rulers and all the people in it. Thus he killed many more when he died than while he lived.
Judges 16:28-30

- Mentioned in: Judges
- Meaning of name: "Sun"
- Lived in: Zorah, a city in Dan (modern day Israel)
- Married to: Unnamed Philistine girl, Delilah
- Father of: Unknown (none mentioned)

Milestones:

Samson was one of the strongest men who ever lived. He used that strength to defend Israel from its enemies, but his weakness was his own selfishness. Unlike Joshua or Gideon, Samson was not a great leader.

Questions:

Sometimes we see power as being big and strong like Samson, but often, power comes in people we least expect. Though Samson was physically strong, he was weak in mind and spirit because he lacked full faith in God. Have you witnessed strength in someone who didn't look strong at first? Have you witnessed people who have faith in God as they overcome big obstacles?

Samson Is Born
Judges 13:1-24

Israel lived in peace for a long time. Then they began to disobey God again. So God let the Philistines rule Israel for forty years. Manoah was an Israelite from the town of Zorah. His wife was not able to have children. One day an angel came to her and said, "God will give you a son. He will belong to the Lord and will help deliver the Israelites from the Philistines. Because of this you must never cut his hair."

The woman ran to Manoah and said, "I have seen an angel! He told me that we are going to have a son!" Manoah prayed to the Lord, "Please let me see the angel, too." When the woman was out in the field, the angel appeared to her again, so she ran back and got her husband, "Come quick," she said. "The angel has returned!" Manoah got up and ran out to the field. The angel said to him, "Your wife must take good care of herself because she will give birth to a special boy."

Manoah and his wife bowed down and worshiped God. They made a sacrifice of a young goat and some grain. As Manoah and his wife watched the sacrifice burn, the angel went up to heaven with the smoke of the offering. When the woman gave birth to a baby boy, she named him Samson. He grew and the Lord blessed him.

Samson Fights a Lion
Judges 14:1-9

One day, when Samson was a young man, he took a trip to the town of Timnah. He saw a Philistine woman there and fell in love with her. When he came home, he told his parents, "I met a Philistine woman I want to marry." "A Philistine!" his parents replied. "Why don't you marry a woman of Israel? The Philistines are our enemies." So his parents went with him to Timnah to arrange the wedding, although they didn't realize the Lord was creating an opportunity to use Samson's strength against the Philistines. As they were walking, Samson wandered off by himself. He saw a lion. The lion chased him and showed his sharp white teeth. Then the Lord's spirit took control of Samson. He tore the lion apart with his bare hands, as if it were a young goat. However, he didn't tell his parents

what had happened. When they arrived, Samson found the Philistine woman. He asked her to marry him. His parents made wedding plans with the bride's family, then Samson and his parents went home.

On their next trip to Timnah for the wedding, Samson went off to take a look at the dead lion. Bees were living inside it and they had made some honey. Samson scooped up the honey in his hands and ate it as he walked along.

Samson and Delilah
Judges 16:4-15

Later, Samson fell in love with another woman, named Delilah. One day, a group of Philistine rulers went to Delilah and said, "How would you like eleven hundred pieces of silver? If you find out what makes Samson so strong, we'll pay you." The next time Delilah saw Samson, she asked, "What makes you so strong?" "Tie me up with seven bowstrings," Samson replied. "Then I'll be just as weak as anyone else." When Samson was asleep, she tied him up. "The Philistines are attacking!" she yelled. He woke up and snapped the bowstrings as easily as if they were threads held over a flame. "Samson! You lied to me. What is it that makes you so strong?" Delilah said. "Okay, tie me with ropes that have never been used," said Samson, "then I'll be weak." While he was asleep, Delilah tied him with new ropes. "The Philistines are attacking!" she yelled, but Samson snapped the ropes off again as if they were threads. "Stop making me look like a fool," Delilah said. "Tell me the truth." "Weave my braided hair on a loom," Samson told her. "Nail the loom to a wall and you'll see how weak I become." When Samson was asleep she weaved his hair on a loom and nailed it to the wall. "The Philistines are attacking!" she yelled. Samson jumped up and all his hair came loose from the loom nailed to the wall. So Delilah said, "Samson, I don't think you love me. You have lied to me three times!"

Delilah Tricks Samson
Judges 16:16-22

Delilah nagged and prodded Samson until he told her the truth. "The Lord makes me strong," he said. "My hair has never been cut. As long as my hair is uncut, I will always be strong." So Delilah went to the Philistines and said, "I know what makes Samson strong! Come to my house tonight while he is asleep." The Philistines paid Delilah the money they had promised her. Then they came to her house after Samson had fallen asleep. He was laying his head in Delilah's lap. She told the Philistines to come and shave off his hair. After they had done this, they tied Samson up with ropes. Then Delilah yelled, "Samson, the Philistines are attacking!" Samson jumped up and tried to break loose from the ropes. He didn't realize the Lord had left him. All his strength was gone. The Philistines poked out his eyes so that he was blind. They put shackles on him and forced him to work as a slave. Samson was miserable. But, little by little, his hair began to grow again.

Samson Pulls Down a Temple
Judges 16:23-30

One day, the Philistine rulers were having a party in their temple, thanking their god, Dagon, that Samson had been overcome. They were eating, drinking, and having a good time. Someone shouted, "Bring out Samson; he's always a good laugh!" A guard brought Samson out to the main room, and they made him perform. Samson asked the guard, "Please lead me in between the two main pillars so I can rest against them." The guard led him toward the two pillars that were holding up the roof. About three thousand Philistines had been watching him perform. Samson prayed to God, "Make me strong one last time. Let me have my revenge on these Philistines for poking out my eyes." Then Samson stretched out his arms and pressed against the two pillars. They began to tremble and shake. "Let me die with the Philistines!" Samson prayed as he pushed with all his might. The pillars crumbled and roof caved in, crushing all the Philistines.

David

David said to the Philistine, "You come against me with sword and spear and javelin, but I come against you in the name of the Lord Almighty, the God of the armies of Israel, whom you have defied.
1 Sam 17:45

- Mentioned in: Ruth, 1 Samuel, 1 Kings, Psalms (David partially wrote), Matthew, Mark, Luke, Acts, Romans, Hebrews
- Meaning of name: "Beloved"
- Lived in: Bethlehem in Judah (modern day Israel), Jerusalem (when he was king)
- Married to: Michal (Saul's daughter), Ahinoam, Abigail, Maacah, Haggith, Abital, Eglah, Bathsheba (mother of Solomon)
- Father of: Amnon (son of Ahinoam), Kilav (son of Abigail), Absalom (son of Maacah), Solomon (son of Bathsheba), Tamar (daughter of Maacah), many others

Milestones:

David's life is full of accomplishments, from defeating Goliath the Giant, to succeeding Saul as King of Israel. He was beloved of God, wrote many psalms in praise of God, and helped raise another future king of Israel, King Solomon, who would be known as the wisest man who ever lived. He also is the direct ancestor of Jesus Christ, who was also known as the "Son of David."

Questions:

- David's life teaches us that we can be great and successful, but also make mistakes. God loved David so much because even though he made mistakes—even some very big ones—he was always humble before God in asking for forgiveness. Can you remember a time when you had to humble yourself before God and ask for forgiveness? How did that make you feel?

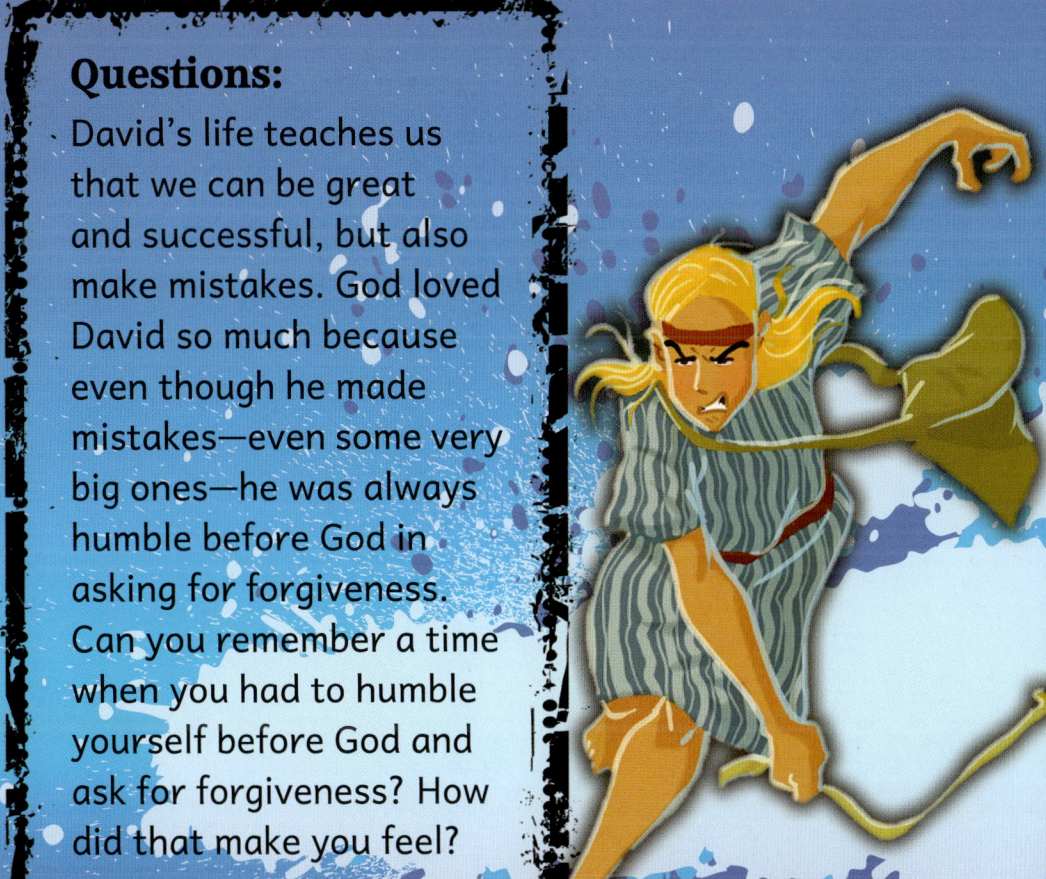

David and Saul
1 Samuel 16:14-23

God had chosen Saul to be the first king of Israel. After several years, Saul no longer obeyed God's commands, and God's Spirit left him. Since God was no longer with him, Saul had been taken over by an evil spirit that would not give him peace. At night, Saul often awoke with horrible nightmares. During the day, he wrestled with bad thoughts.

One day when Saul was feeling particularly bad, his servants sent for a musician to come and play music to calm him down.

David was still a young man, but he played the harp very well. Saul's servants heard good things about David, so they hired him to play the harp for Saul. When David plucked the strings of his instrument, a peaceful melody filled the air. His music seemed

to come from heaven. Saul immediately relaxed, and the bad spirit left him. Saul loved David very much, but sometimes he was so angry and jealous that he would try to kill him.

Goliath the Giant
1 Samuel 17:3-11

The Philistines were planning an attack on the people of Israel. King Saul commanded all his best men to prepare for battle. They took up their spears, and walked toward the battlefield with confidence. Then they saw Goliath. Goliath was the hero of the Philistine army. He was huge! He towered over the other men like a fierce giant. His legs were as thick as tree trunks, and his arms bulged with muscles. Goliath laughed and snorted at the army of Israel. When he spoke, his words sounded like a beastly roar. "I am the best soldier of our army," Goliath shouted. "If one among you can kill me, the Philistines will be your slaves. But if I kill him, all of Israel will be our slaves!" He shouted like that every morning and evening for forty days. Saul and his men were terrified. Even the bravest among the soldiers of Israel began to shake with fright.

David Meets Goliath
1 Samuel 17:12-16; 34-40

David's three oldest brothers were in Saul's army. One day, David's father sent him with some food for his brothers. He arrived at the army just as Goliath was shouting his threats.

David went up to Saul and said, "I have killed lions and bears when they have dared to attack my sheep. Now let me fight Goliath who has dared to insult the army of the living God." But Saul was not so sure about this. Still, he admired David and gave him his armor and sword to use.

David put on the heavy armor and iron helmet, but he was uncomfortable. "I can't move with this on," he said. David threw off the armor and instead, picked up his shepherd's staff. Then he chose five smooth stones from a stream and put them into his shepherd's bag. With his sling in his hand, he went straight toward Goliath.

David Kills Goliath
1 Samuel 17:41-51

Goliath howled with laughter when he saw David. He said, "Do you think I am a dog? Are you going to come after me with a stick?" But David answered bravely, "You come against me with sword, spear and javelin, but I come against you in the name of the Lord Almighty!" Then David

ran at Goliath and slung a rock at him with his slingshot. It hit Goliath right in the forehead. Goliath wobbled and swayed with dizziness then he fell down onto the ground with a thud. Quickly, David took Goliath's sword, killed him, and cut off his head. Israel was saved! David had become a hero.

Elijah

Answer me, Lord, answer me, so these people will know that you, Lord, are God, and that you are turning their hearts back again." Then the fire of the Lord fell and burned up the sacrifice, the wood, the stones and the soil, and also licked up the water in the trench.
1 Kings 18:37-38

- Mentioned in: 1 Kings, 2 Kings, 2 Chronicles, Malachi, Matthew, Luke, John, Romans, James
- Meaning of name: "My God is YAHWEH"
- Lived in: Tishbe in Gilead (modern day Jordan), Kerith Valley (modern day Israel), Zarephath (modern day Lebanon), many other places in Israel and Judah
- Married to: None mentioned
- Father of: None mentioned

Milestones:

Elijah was a powerful prophet who performed miracles in God's name. He helped do away with false gods, which people began to worship after King Solomon's death. Instead of dying, Elijah was taken directly up to heaven in a chariot with horses of fire.

Questions:

There are many false gods in our world today: money, fame, and possessions, to name a few. Anything that takes the place of God can be considered an idol. Which things in your life could potentially be "idols," and how can you avoid them turning into idols?

Elijah in the Wilderness
1 Kings 16:32-33; 17:1-7

Many years later, when David's son, Solomon, died, the kingdom was divided into two. The northern part, called Israel, and the southern part, called Judah. King after king did evil things. It was King Ahab of Israel who angered God more than any of the other kings. He disobeyed God by worshiping idols and setting up an altar to Baal.

Elijah was a prophet. He went to King Ahab and told him, "I serve the Lord, God. The Lord has sent me to tell you that it won't rain until I say so. For the next few years, there won't even be dew on the ground." Then God told Elijah to go and hide near Cherith brook, east of the Jordan River. "You can drink from the brook," the Lord told him, "and I will send the ravens to bring you food." So Elijah obeyed the Lord and lived in the wilderness. He drank the water from the brook. Every morning and evening, ravens came to Elijah bringing him bread and meat. When the brook dried up, God sent him somewhere else.

The True God
1 Kings 18:16-39

After three and one half years, God told Elijah to go to King Ahab and tell him that the Lord would send rain. When King Ahab heard that Elijah was coming, he ran out to meet him. "You troublemaker," he yelled, "look at all the suffering you've caused Israel!" Elijah told him, "You are the troublemaker. You have disobeyed God and worshiped Baal. Let's sacrifice two bulls. You can sacrifice your bull to Baal. I'll sacrifice my bull to the Lord, God. But, we won't light any fire, instead, we will pray. Let the true God answer our prayer by sending fire." So Elijah and King Ahab prepared the two bulls and put them on the altars. King Ahab brought out his prophets. They danced around the bull. "Answer us, Baal!" they prayed. Nothing happened all morning. "Pray louder!" Elijah teased them, "Maybe he's taking a nap, and you have to wake him up." Many hours later, Elijah finally went over to his altar. First, he made sure to pour water over the sacrifice until the water gathered in a trench around the altar. "Lord, please answer me," Elijah prayed. "Let these people know that You are God. Then, they will give their hearts back to You." King Ahab and all his prophets watched as fire came from heaven and swallowed up the sacrifice. Even

the water in the trench had been licked up by the fire. King Ahab and his men fell to the ground and said, "The Lord is God!" Then God sent rain!

Daniel

Daniel answered, "May the king live forever! My God sent his angel, and he shut the mouths of the lions. They have not hurt me, because I was found innocent in his sight. Nor have I ever done any wrong before you, Your Majesty."
Dan 6:21-22

- Mentioned in: Daniel, Matthew
- Meaning of name: "God is my judge"
- Lived in: Jerusalem (modern day Israel), Babylon (modern day Iraq) taken here as captive when young man
- Married to: None mentioned
- Father of: None mentioned

Milestones:

Daniel was a trusted advisor of Babylonian kings, and even though he worked in the Babylonian court, he kept his Jewish faith and loved God his entire life. Like Joseph before him, God gave him the meaning of people's dreams. He also gained people's respect by being honest and upfront.

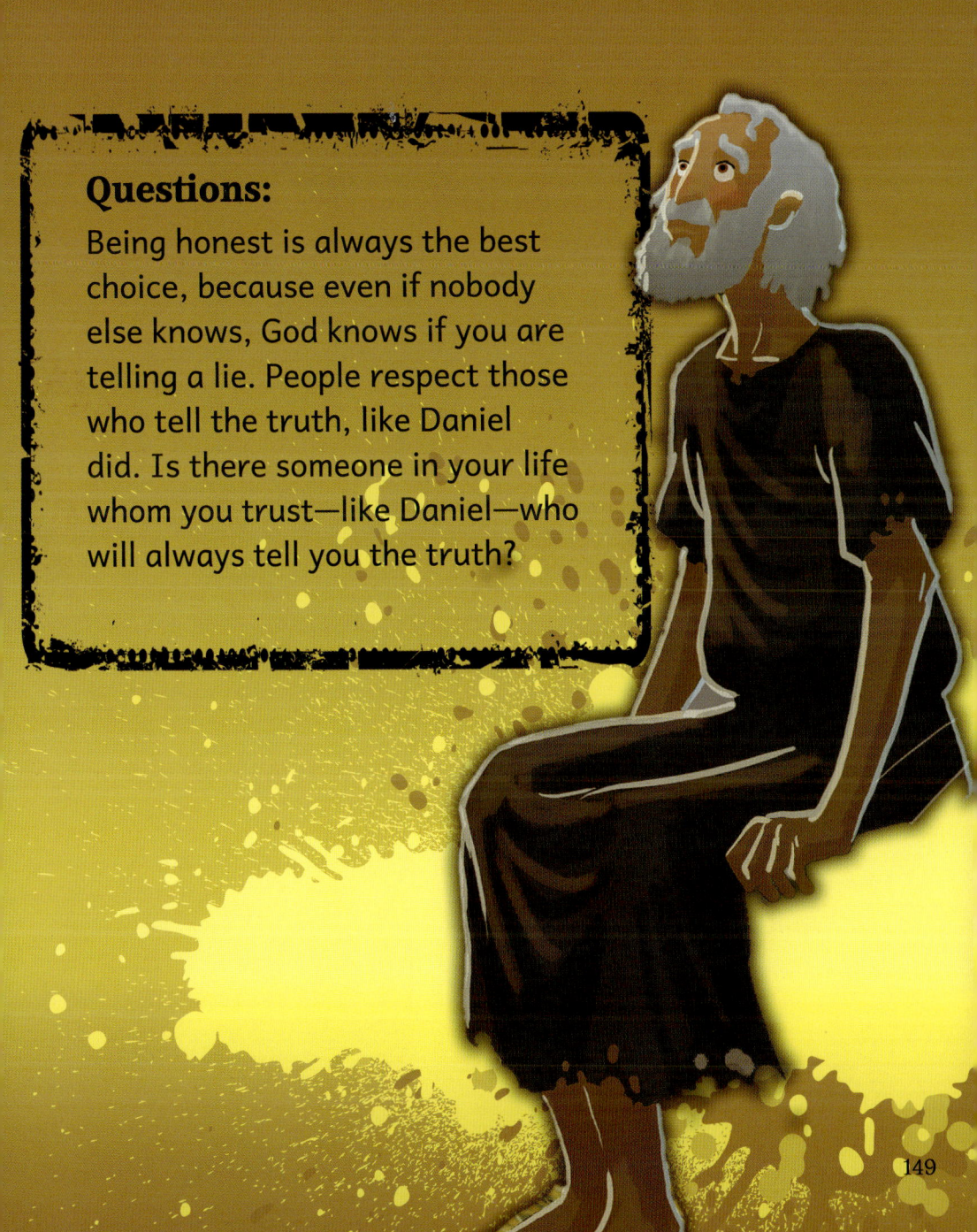

Questions:

Being honest is always the best choice, because even if nobody else knows, God knows if you are telling a lie. People respect those who tell the truth, like Daniel did. Is there someone in your life whom you trust—like Daniel—who will always tell you the truth?

Daniel and His Friends
Daniel 1:3-7

The kings of Judah also disobeyed God, so He allowed King Nebuchadnezzar to invade the land and carry the Israelites into captivity in Babylon. Not all of the Israelites became slaves. The king ordered his chief official to pick some of them to come and work in his palace. "Make sure they are healthy, smart, and handsome," he told him. "I only want the very best working for me." Then he said, "They must be turned into Babylonians. Teach them our language, and make sure they read all our books. After three years of training, they can work for me." So the king's official went to the Israelites. He tested their strength and their smarts. When he had finally picked out the best ones, he brought them back to the king's palace. The king

refused to let them keep their Jewish names. He gave them each a Babylonian name instead. Daniel was one of the young men chosen, but they changed his name to Belteshazzar. Daniel's three friends were also chosen. They were renamed Shadrach, Meshach, and Abednego.

A Test of Faith
Daniel 1:8-21

Daniel and his three friends were given food and wine from the king's table. Because some of it was what the Israelites called unclean, they asked to be given only vegetables and water. Their guard agreed to let them try. After ten days, Daniel and his friends were stronger and healthier looking than any of the other men, so the guard

let them continue to eat only vegetables and water. They never became weak, instead they grew stronger and more intelligent. They read every book in the palace and knew many things. Daniel also had the gift of telling the meaning of dreams. The king was so impressed with the four young men that he gave them high positions in the royal court.

Nebuchadnezzar's Dream
Daniel 2:1-13

King Nebuchadnezzar began to wake up with horrible nightmares. For several nights, he dreamed the same thing. Sweat poured from his forehead, and he was afraid to shut his eyes. He summoned his best magicians and some of his wise men. "I am very upset about my dream," he told them, "I don't know what it means." "Tell us what it was about," they said, "and maybe we can tell you the

meaning." The king said, "Aren't you magicians and wise men? You should be able to tell me what I dreamed and its meaning. If you don't, I'll chop you into pieces and tear your houses down. But if you do, then I'll reward you." "That's impossible," they cried, "No one could know that except the gods, and we are not gods." The king became furious. He gave orders for every wise man in Babylonia to be put to death, including Daniel and his three friends!

God Reveals the Dream to Daniel
Daniel 2:19-48

That night, Daniel and his three friends prayed that the Lord would reveal the king's dream to Daniel. And he did! The next day, Daniel went to the king and said: "Your Majesty, no man, no matter how wise, could tell you what your dream meant. Only God knows. Last night, he made your dream known to me. In your dream, you looked up and saw a terrifying statue standing over you. The statue's head was of gold, its chest and arms of silver, its belly and thighs of bronze, its legs of iron, and its feet of both iron and clay. Then you watched a stone being cut away from a mountain. The stone fell on the statue's

feet and the whole thing was crushed and blown away. That was your dream. Now, I will tell you what your dream means. You are the statue's head, made of gold. After you are gone, another kingdom will rule. Then, a kingdom of bronze will rule—and then a kingdom of iron. Lastly, a kingdom divided will rule, just like the feet were a mixture of iron and clay. The stone that destroyed the statue is the kingdom that the God of heaven will raise up. A kingdom that will never be destroyed." The king was amazed. He told Daniel, "Your God gave you the power to understand my dream. Now I know that your God is the true Lord." So the king made Daniel governor of Babylon.

King Belshazzar's Banquet
Daniel 5:1–12

King Belshazzar ruled over Babylon after his father, Nebuchadnezzar, died. One evening, he threw a party at his palace. He had a feast prepared and set a long beautiful table. He ordered only the best gold and silver cups to be used. So, they used the cups taken from the temple in Jerusalem. All of the king's highest officials were invited. They ate and drank and praised their idols made of gold and silver, bronze, iron, wood, and stone. While they were busy having a good time, a hand suddenly appeared and began writing on the wall of the palace. The king turned as white as a ghost, and his knees began to knock together because he was so frightened. Pointing to the writing, "What does this say?" the king asked his advisors. "Whoever can read this will be the third most powerful man in Babylon. He can wear purple robes and a gold chain and live like royalty." The king's highest officials studied the writing but they couldn't understand a word of it. Then, the queen mother came in and heard the men talking. She said, "Don't look so scared. There is one man who can explain dreams and solve riddles like this. Don't you remember Daniel? Bring him in here and he'll solve the mystery for you."

Daniel Reads the Writing
Daniel 5:13-31

Daniel was brought before the king. "I hear that you have great insight and wisdom," the king said to him. "If you can read me the writing on the wall and tell me what it means, I will make you very rich." "Your Majesty," Daniel replied, "I will tell you what the writing means, but keep all your jewels and fancy robes. I don't want them. The Most High God gave your father power and riches, but his heart became proud. Therefore, he lost everything and he was given the mind of an animal. He lived among the animals and ate grass until he humbled himself and learned that God rules all the kingdoms of the world and chooses the kings He wants. You knew all this and still you are following in his footsteps, Your Majesty. You are using the cups from God's temple to drink wine with your friends and toast to your idols and statues. That's why God has sent this hand to write on the wall. The words written here mean: numbered, weighed, and divided. God has numbered your days. He has weighed your time in power, and you fall short of doing a good job. He is also going to divide your kingdom between the Medes and the Persians." So the king sent Daniel away keeping his promise to make him the third most powerful man in Babylon. That very night the king was killed by Darius the Mede, who took over as king.

Daniel in the Lion's Pit
Daniel 6:1-28

King Darius divided his kingdom and put leaders in charge of each part. After he discovered how wise Daniel was, he made him head of all the other leaders. The other leaders were very jealous of Daniel. They tried to find something to accuse him of, but Daniel was an honest man, and he always did excellent work. "Maybe we can trick Daniel into getting in trouble," they schemed. They went to Darius and said, "Why don't you make a law that, for the next thirty days, any person who prays to anyone, except to Your Majesty, will be thrown into the den of lions." King Darius agreed and put the law in writing. Daniel heard about the law, but he went home that night and prayed to God, just like he had always done. Just outside his door, there were spies. They saw Daniel praying and ran back to the king. "Your Majesty," they cried, "Daniel disobeyed you. He's in his house praying to his God." King Darius was deeply troubled by this and all day he tried to find a way to save Daniel. At last he said, "I can't take back what I have put in the law." So Daniel was taken away and thrown into a pit full of hungry lions. A stone was rolled over the pit and he was left so no one could rescue him.

That night, Darius couldn't sleep. He kept thinking about Daniel in the lion's den. As soon as the sun came up, Darius ran back to the pit to see what had happened. He rolled away the stone. "Daniel, has your God saved you?" he yelled into the darkness. "Yes, Your Majesty," Daniel answered. "God sent an angel to keep the lions from hurting me, because He knew I was innocent." So the king had Daniel taken out of the pit. He didn't even have a scratch on him! God had protected him because of his faithfulness. Darius ordered all the men who had plotted against Daniel to be thrown into the pit, and the hungry lions crushed them before they even touched the bottom.

The New Testament

An Angel Visits Mary
Luke 1:26-38

The angel Gabriel went to the town of Nazareth. He had a message for a young woman named Mary. "Greetings," he told her, "You are truly blessed!" but Mary was frightened. She had never seen an angel before and didn't understand what he was talking about. "Don't be afraid. The Lord is with you," the angel said. "He has sent me to tell you that you will give birth to a son. He will be called the Son of God. God will make Him a king just like His ancestor David, but His kingdom will never end."

"How can I have a child?" Mary asked him. "I'm not married."

The angel answered, "The Holy Spirit will make it happen. That's why the child will be called the Son of God. Nothing is impossible for God! Even your relative Elizabeth, who is barren, is going to have a child in her old age."

"I am God's servant," Mary said. "I will do whatever He wants." Then the angel Gabriel left her.

Joseph

But after he had considered this, an angel of the Lord appeared to him in a dream and said, "Joseph son of David, do not be afraid to take Mary home as your wife, because what is conceived in her is from the Holy Spirit. She will give birth to a son, and you are to give him the name Jesus, because he will save his people from their sins."
Matt 1:20-21

- Mentioned in: Matthew, Luke
- Meaning of name: "To increase"
- Lived in: Nazareth, a city in Galilee (modern day Israel), Egypt, back to Nazareth
- Married to: Mary (Mother of Jesus)
- Father of: James, Joses, Judas, Simon, daughters
- Stepfather of: Jesus

Milestones:

Joseph was a kind and caring man, who was gentle and understanding to his wife and children. God chose Joseph for a reason: his temperament, character, and faith made him the perfect choice to be Jesus' earthly father.

Questions:

God entrusted Joseph with raising His only son. Have you ever entrusted someone with something important? Was that person someone you could trust like Joseph, who was of high moral character?

What, in your opinion, makes a person trustworthy?

Joseph's Dream
Matthew 1:18-24

Mary was engaged to a carpenter, named Joseph. He was a good man, and he loved Mary very much. After she told him about the angel's visit and he realized she was pregnant, Joseph decided to break the engagement quietly and not expose her to public shame. That night, while Joseph was asleep, an angel came and spoke to him. "Joseph," the angel said, "it's true that Mary's baby will be the Son of God, but don't call off your wedding. Marry her and raise the child together. His name will be Jesus, and He will save people from their sins." Joseph woke up and did what the angel had told him to do and took Mary as his wife.

Jesus Is Born
Luke 2:1-7

The Emperor of Rome had ordered that everyone must list their families in the record books. People had to register in their hometown, so Joseph left Nazareth and went to Bethlehem, the hometown of his ancestor King David. Mary came with him. It was almost time for her to give birth.

By the time they arrived, it was late, and they were tired. Since so many people had come to register, there was no room to be found, so Joseph and Mary had to stay in a stable. That night, Mary gave birth to Jesus. She wrapped

Him in cloths so He wouldn't be cold. She made a little bed of hay and laid Jesus down on it.

The Shepherds
Luke 2:8-20

That night, shepherds were out in the fields with their sheep. Suddenly, the angel of the Lord came and showered them with light. They were frightened and hid their faces. "Don't be afraid," the angel said. "I have brought good news. Today in King David's town a baby has been born. He is Christ the Lord. Go and worship Him. You'll find Him asleep on a bed of hay." Suddenly, the angel of the Lord was joined by other angels, all singing praises to God. "Praise God in heaven," they sang. "He gives His peace to people on earth who will receive it." Then, they left and went back to God. The shepherds were alone in the dark night, but the light still twinkled in their eyes. "Let's go and see what the angel was talking about," they said to each other.

They went to Bethlehem and found Jesus asleep on the hay. "The angel said that He is Christ the Lord," the shepherds told Mary. They bowed down and worshiped the child. Mary listened to the shepherds and stored up their words like treasures in her heart. The shepherds left, but the whole way home they kept praising the Lord.

The Wise Men
Matthew 2:1-12

After Jesus was born, wise men arrived in Jerusalem in search of Jesus. They went to Herod's palace and asked, "Where is the newborn king of the Jews? We have seen His star in the East, and we have come to worship Him." King Herod was terrified! A new king? He asked his advisors where the Messiah would be born. "In Bethlehem," they said. So, King Herod told the wise men, "Go to Bethlehem. Search for the child, and when you find Him, come back and tell me. I want to go and worship Him too."

The wise men followed the bright star until it stopped over the place where Jesus lived with Mary and Joseph.

When the wise men saw baby Jesus, they knelt down to worship Him, and laid their gifts at His feet. They had brought gold, frankincense and myrrh from their country in the East.

That night, while the wise men were asleep, an angel warned them in a dream not to go back to King Herod. So the wise men returned home by a different road.

Jesus of Nazareth
Matthew 2:13-23; Luke 2:40

King Herod waited for the wise men to come back and tell him where Jesus lived, but they never came. He thought they had tricked him, and he became furious. He did not want Jesus to grow up and become a rival king to him. He ordered his soldiers to kill all baby boys in Bethlehem. That night, an angel came to Joseph in a dream. "Get up!" the angel said. "Take the child and his mother and flee to Egypt. King Herod is looking for Jesus. He wants to kill Him!" Joseph immediately jumped out of bed and woke up Mary. They loaded their donkey with the few things they owned and left for Egypt.

Sometime later, an angel came to Joseph again in a dream. "It's safe to return to Israel," the angel told him. "King Herod has died, and there is no more danger." The angel told Joseph not to return to Bethlehem. So Joseph and Mary went back to Nazareth and raised Jesus in that town where He grew up healthy and happy.

Jesus in the Temple
Luke 2:41-52

Mary and Joseph went to Jerusalem every year for Passover. When Jesus was twelve, He came with them. After the celebration was over, Mary and Joseph got ready to go back to Nazareth. They thought Jesus was with some of their friends traveling back, too. Their friends said, "No, we haven't seen Him." Mary started to panic, "Oh no, we've lost Him," she cried. They began to search all over Jerusalem.

Three days later, they found Jesus in the temple. He was talking with the teachers and asking them questions.

Everyone in the temple was amazed by His wisdom.

"Son," Mary cried out when she saw Him, "why did You scare us like this? We've been looking for You everywhere!"

Jesus replied, "Why did you have to look? Didn't you know that I would be in My Father's house?" Then He went with His parents back to Nazareth, and Mary kept thinking about what Jesus had said.

John the Baptist

John replied in the words of Isaiah the prophet, "I am the voice of one calling in the wilderness, 'Make straight the way for the Lord.'"
John 1:23

- Mentioned in: Isaiah, Malachi, Matthew, Mark, Luke, John, Acts
- Meaning of name: "Grace" or "Mercy of God"
- Lived in: Wilderness of Judea, (modern day Israel)
- Married to: None mentioned
- Father of: None mentioned

Milestones:

Jesus called John the Baptist the greatest of the Old Testament prophets. What made John so great? His unique and most important task was to prepare the way for Jesus, the Lamb of God who takes away the sin of the world. He baptized people who confessed and turned from their sins. He also baptized Jesus in the river Jordan. He was brave. He feared no one but God Himself, so he was killed for challenging the mighty King Herod to stop sinning.

> **Questions:**
> Not all of us can be as brave as John the Baptist, but if we have faith in God, our fears can be far less frightening. Can you name a brave person in your life? Was there a time when you had to overcome your fears and be brave?

John the Baptist
Luke 1:5-25; John 1:19-28

Before Mary was told she would be expecting Jesus, the angel Gabriel also visited a priest, named Zechariah, in the temple in Jerusalem. The angel promised him and his wife, Elizabeth, a son though she was past childbearing age. Elizabeth was a relative of Mary. But God kept His promise, and Elizabeth had a son whom she named

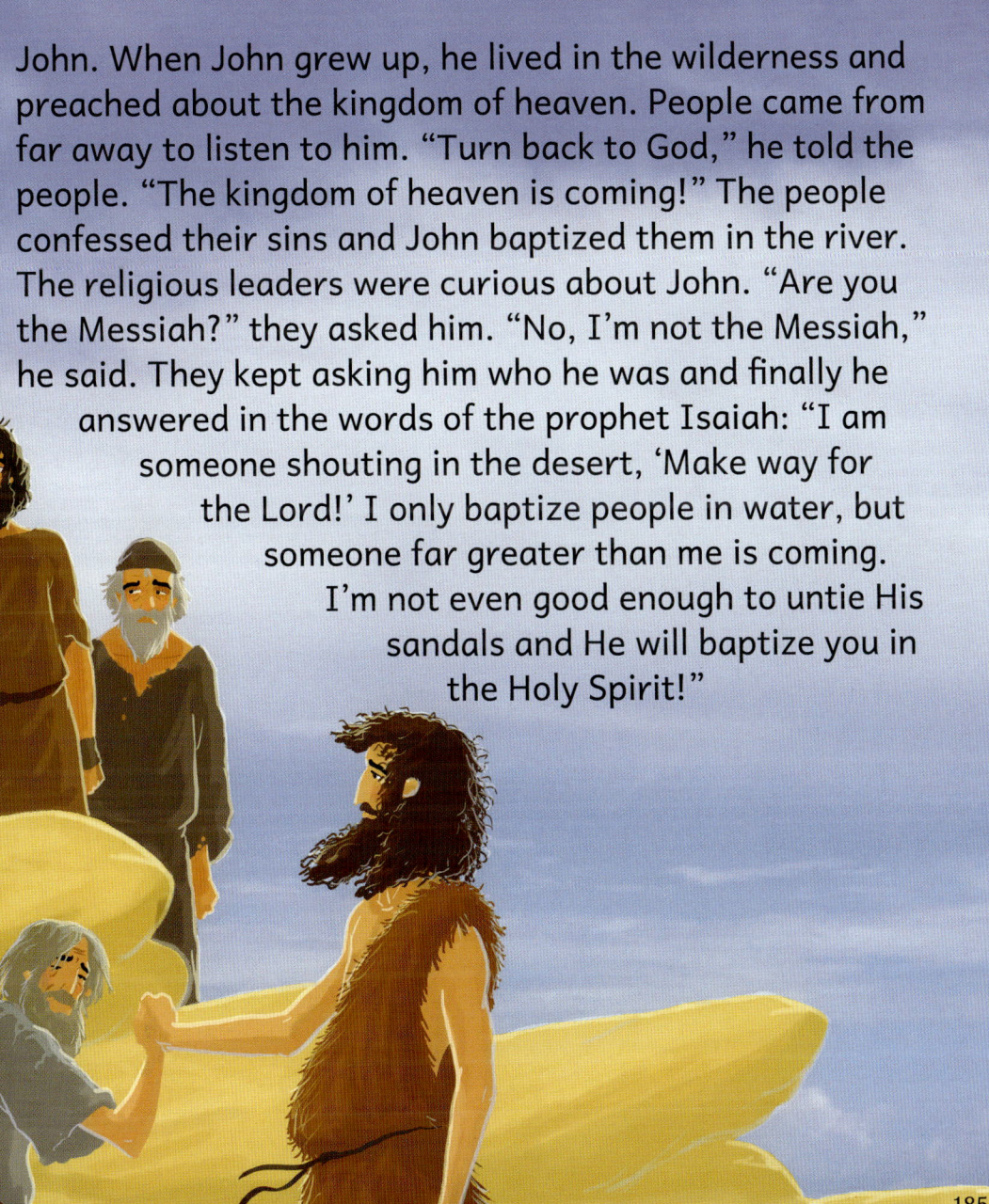

John. When John grew up, he lived in the wilderness and preached about the kingdom of heaven. People came from far away to listen to him. "Turn back to God," he told the people. "The kingdom of heaven is coming!" The people confessed their sins and John baptized them in the river. The religious leaders were curious about John. "Are you the Messiah?" they asked him. "No, I'm not the Messiah," he said. They kept asking him who he was and finally he answered in the words of the prophet Isaiah: "I am someone shouting in the desert, 'Make way for the Lord!' I only baptize people in water, but someone far greater than me is coming. I'm not even good enough to untie His sandals and He will baptize you in the Holy Spirit!"

Jesus Is Baptized
Matthew 3:13-16; John 1:29-35

One day, Jesus came to be baptized, too. But John refused saying, "Jesus, you should be the one baptizing me!"

"It is right for us to do this. It carries out God's holy plan," Jesus answered. So John baptized Jesus in the Jordan River. As Jesus lifted his head from the water, the sky opened up. The Spirit of God came down from heaven like a dove, and the voice of God said,

"This is My beloved Son, and I am pleased with Him."

The next day, John saw Jesus coming toward him. John turned to the people and said, "This is the man I told you about when I said, 'He is greater than I am.' He is the Lamb of God, the one who takes away your sins."

Then John said, "I have known Jesus all my life. He is my relative, but I didn't realize He was the one until yesterday. God, who sent me to baptize with water, told me, 'The one on whom you see the Spirit descend upon and rest is the one who will baptize with the Holy Spirit.'"

The Devil Tempts Jesus
Luke 4:1-15

After His baptism, Jesus was led by the Holy Spirit into the desert. Jesus stayed in the desert for forty days and forty nights. He didn't eat anything, so He was very hungry. The devil was there, too, so he tried to trick Jesus into disobeying God.

"If You're the Son of God," the devil told him, "You should be able to turn this stone into a delicious loaf of bread. Think how good it will taste!"

Jesus answered, "No one can live on food alone. It is God's word that gives life!"

Then, the devil led Jesus

to the peak of a very high mountain. He showed Him all the nations of the world. "You can be the ruler over everything. All You have to do is to kneel down and worship me," the devil told Him.

Jesus answered, "God's word tells us to worship Him only."

So the devil took Jesus to the highest place at the temple in Jerusalem. "If You're the Son of God, jump off. The angels will surely catch You."

Jesus answered, "God's word tells us we must not test Him."

Then, the devil went away. Jesus had stayed true to God. After His time in the desert, Jesus went back home to Galilee.

Peter

"Lord, if it's you," Peter replied, "tell me to come to you on the water." "Come," he said. Then Peter got down out of the boat, walked on the water and came toward Jesus.
Matt 14:28-29

- Mentioned in: Matthew, Mark, Luke, John, Galatians, He wrote 1 Peter , 2 Peter
- Meaning of name: "Rock" --Hebrew birth name Simon ("listener") was changed by Jesus
- Lived in: Bethsaida in Galilee (modern day Israel), many places after Jesus died, even Rome (where he was crucified)
- Married to: Unknown
- Father of: Unknown

Milestones:

Peter was a very bold and very loyal man, and these are the qualities that Jesus saw when He met him. Jesus knew that Peter would help spread the Word of God. However, Peter was also a fearful man, and he denied Jesus three times. Jesus forgave Peter and told him to use the same talents he used as a disciple to go forth and spread the Word.

Questions:

No one is perfect, and Jesus knew that. Even though Jesus Himself, the Son of God, was a perfect human being on earth, He knows that humans have faults. Peter had his faults, but he also had great strengths. Do you know your strengths? Do you know your weaknesses? There is no shame in admitting them to God and yourself. God is always willing to help you.

Jesus Calls His First Disciples
Matthew 4:18-22

While Jesus was walking along the shore of Lake Galilee, He saw two brothers. One was Simon, called Peter, and the other was his brother, Andrew. They were fishermen, and they were casting their nets into the lake. Jesus said to them, "Come with Me! I will teach you how to catch people instead of fish." Right then, the two brothers dropped their nets and went with Him. Jesus walked on until He saw James and John, the sons of Zebedee. They were in a boat with their father, mending their nets. Jesus asked them to come with Him, too, and right away they left the boat, and their father, and went with Jesus.

Fishers of Men
Luke 5:1-11

Jesus was standing by the Sea of Galilee teaching a crowd of people. Two fishermen's boats were tied up nearby. Jesus got into the boat that belonged to Simon. He told Simon to row a little way out from shore. Jesus then taught from the boat while the people sat on the shore.

When He was finished, He told Simon to row further out into the lake. Simon obeyed. "Now, drop your nets and catch some fish," Jesus said. "Master," Simon replied, "we've been out fishing all night. There was not a single fish to be caught. However, I will do what You say." Simon threw the nets into the water, and they filled up with fish. There were so many fish that the nets began to rip. "We need help!" Simon called to the other fishermen. So James and John rowed the other boat out and helped them haul in the nets. There were so many fish that the boats began to sink! When Simon saw all the fish, he knew that Jesus was God's Son. He fell on his knees before Jesus. "Lord, don't come near me. I'm just a sinner." Jesus told Simon, "Don't be afraid! From now on you will bring in people instead of fish." When the men reached the shore, they left everything to become Jesus' disciples.

Jesus Heals a Crippled Man
Mark 2:1-12, Luke 5:17-26

One day, Jesus was teaching a group of people who had come from all over Israel to meet Him. The crowd gathered into one room, and soon there was no place left to stand or sit. Four men came carrying their paralyzed friend on a mat. There were too many people, so the crippled man did not get to see Jesus. Then, his friends had an idea! They removed some tiles on the roof and lowered the man down through the ceiling.

When Jesus saw how much faith they had, He said to the crippled man, "Friend, your sins are forgiven." The Pharisees heard that and became angry. "Who does He think He is?" they said to each other. "Only God can forgive sins." Jesus looked at them and said, "Why

do you say such things? What is easiest? To forgive his sins or tell him to start walking? So that you will know that the Son of Man has been given authority to forgive sins, I say: Pick up your mat and walk home!" The man began to stand up. His crippled legs had been healed, and he could walk!

People were amazed and they praised God saying, "We have seen a miracle today!"

Planting Seeds
Mark 4:1-20

While Jesus was teaching by the Sea of Galilee, He told this story: "A farmer went out to scatter his seeds. Some seeds fell on the road, but the birds came and ate them. Some seeds fell between the rocks. They sprouted but quickly died because there was not enough deep soil to grow strong roots. Some seeds fell among the thorn bushes and were choked as they started to grow. However, some of the farmer's seeds fell on good ground. These seeds turned into a great harvest, 30 to 100 times more than what had been planted."

The disciples didn't understand the meaning of Jesus' story, so He explained it to them. "Some people are like the seeds on the road. They hear My words, but then the devil comes and takes it away from them. Some are like the seeds falling between the rocks; they believe, but when they suffer hardships because of their faith, they fall away. The seeds being choked by the thorn bushes are like

people who believe, but let worries and desires for wealth and riches choke their faith. But, others are like the seeds sown on good ground. They hear My word and live by it. Through them, many people will follow My Father also."

True Happiness
Matthew 5:1-12

Jesus went up to the side of the mountain where all the people had gathered to hear Him speak.

"My friends," Jesus said, "God blesses those who look to Him for help. They belong to the kingdom of heaven! God blesses those who feel sad and hopeless. He will comfort them! God blesses those who are humble. They belong to God! God blesses

those who obey Him. They will be given what they ask for! God blesses those who are forgiving and show mercy to others. They will be treated with forgiveness and mercy! God blesses those whose hearts are pure. They will see Him! God blesses those who make peace. They will be called His children! God blesses those who are treated badly for doing what is right. They too belong to God's kingdom! Be happy! Feel excited and joyful today! For those who do what is right by God will have a big reward in the kingdom of heaven."

Being Salt and Light
Matthew 5:13-16

Jesus said to His friends, "You are the salt of the earth. What would salt be like if it didn't taste salty? You might as well throw it out and walk over it. You, too, will be useless unless you do as you should. Forgive the people that do you wrong. Love each other. Share what you have with others."

After a pause, Jesus continued, "You are the shining light that illuminates the world. No one would light a lamp and put it under a clay pot, would they? All the light would be hidden, and no one could see. A lamp is placed on a lamp stand where it can give light to everything in the house. Let your light shine bright. Share your light with others. They will see the good you do, and they will give praise to your Father in heaven."

Do Not Worry
Matthew 6:19-30

One morning, Jesus was speaking to a large crowd that had gathered outside.

He said, "All the things you have here on earth are of little worth. A moth can come and chew your clothes. Rust can ruin your favorite things and thieves can come and steal your money. Don't store up these things that can be taken from you. Treasures in heaven cannot be destroyed or taken from you. Give your heart to God alone! You cannot love riches and God at the same time. Have faith that God will take care of you. He will give you everything you need."

"Look at the birds in the sky. Aren't they cheerful and happy? They don't work all the time, and yet God takes care of them! Look at the wildflowers. They don't worry

about clothes, yet even Solomon didn't look as fine and colorful as they do! God takes care of everything that grows, even if it only lives for a day. If He does that for the birds and the flowers, He will certainly take care of you, too."

The House on the Rock
Matthew 7:24-29

Jesus said, "Anyone who hears and obeys these teachings of Mine is like the wise man who built his house on solid rock. Rain poured down, rivers rose up, and winds beat against that house. Why did it stay standing? Because it was built on firm ground! Obey My teachings

and they will be like a solid rock for you." Anyone who hears My teachings and still disobeys will be like the foolish man who built his house on sand. Rain poured down, rivers rose up, and winds beat against that house, and it crumbled right to the ground. The foolish man does not remain strong when problems come upon him because he does not depend on God."

The Storm
Mark 4:35-38

Jesus was with His disciples on the Sea of Galilee. The sky was growing dark and Jesus said, "Let's cross to the other side." While they were crossing, a storm started to blow. Waves splashed and filled the inside of the boat with water. The boat got heavier and heavier and was about to sink.

"Jesus, help us!" the disciples cried. However, Jesus was asleep at the back of the boat. He didn't hear them. The storm was growing worse, so they woke Him up. "Teacher," they said, "don't You care that we drown?"

Jesus Calms the Storm
Mark 4:39-41

When Jesus woke up, He didn't panic like the disciples. He stood up and held out His hand.

He told the waves, "Be quiet!" He told the wind, "Be still!" All at once, the sea stopped thrashing and the wind stopped howling. It was calm and peaceful again.

Jesus turned back around to His disciples and said, "Why were you afraid? Don't you have faith?"

The disciples were terrified and asked each other: "Who is this man? Even the wind and the waves obey Him!"

Jesus Seeks a Quiet Place
Mark 6:30-33

The disciples were sitting with Jesus. They were telling Him about their day and all the things they had done and taught. People were walking by with noisy carts and animals. Jesus said, "Let's go find a quiet place where we can be alone and get some rest."

They left town and went down to the lake. They got into their boat to look for a quiet place, but the people from town saw them leave and said to each other, "Come on. Let's follow Jesus!" People from other villages left what they were doing and came, too. A few of them had an idea of where Jesus and the disciples were going, so the whole crowd ran ahead and got there first. There were over five thousand people!

The Hungry People
Mark 6:34-38; John 6:5-9

When the disciples saw the big crowd, they groaned. But Jesus didn't mind, He felt compassion for them. They were like sheep without a shepherd. He told them to come closer, and He began to teach. Afternoon rolled around and the disciples were hungry. "Let's take a break," they told Jesus. "The people can go back to their villages and

eat something." Jesus said, "Why don't you give them something to eat?" "That's impossible," they replied. "It would cost a fortune to feed all these people!" The disciple Andrew said, "Well, there is a boy here with some food. He has five loaves of bread and two fish, but that's not enough to feed five thousand people."

Five Loaves and Two Fish
Matthew 14:13-21, Mark 6:39-44, Luke 9:10-17, John 6:10-14

Jesus told His disciples to have faith. "Tell the people to find a nice spot in the grass and sit down," He said. So the disciples obeyed. Once the people quieted down, Jesus stood up, took a loaf of bread in His hands, and gave thanks to God. He then broke the bread and gave it to the disciples, who passed it around to the people. He

continued until every single person had a piece. Then He did the same with the fish.

There was plenty of food, and the people couldn't eat it all. Jesus told His disciples to not let anything go to waste. So they went around and gathered up the extra food in big baskets. The people were amazed when they saw Jesus' miracle. "How did He make so much food out of so little?" they wondered. "It was a miracle! He must be the Prophet whom God has promised to send to the world!"

Jesus Walks on Water
Matthew 14:22-32, Mark 6:45-52

When the day was done, Jesus told His disciples to go home without Him. He wanted to be by Himself for a while. They said goodbye and got in their boat. When all the crowds had left, Jesus climbed up to the side of the mountain and prayed.

That evening, Jesus was still by Himself on the mountainside. He could see the lake from where He sat,

and He spotted His disciples in their boat. The wind was very strong and they were having trouble rowing. So Jesus went down to help them. He started to walk on top of the water toward them. But when the disciples saw Him, they were scared. "It's a ghost!" they cried out. They clung to each other's arms and trembled. "It's me!" Jesus told them. "Don't be afraid."

Peter Lacks Faith
Matthew 14:28-32

Peter said, "Lord, if it's really You, then let me walk out to You on the water." Jesus answered, "Come here, Peter. Don't be afraid." Peter walked toward the edge of the boat. Then, he stepped out onto the waves. He didn't sink, so he began to walk toward Jesus. Then the wind picked up, and Peter got nervous. He started to

look down at his feet. "I'm sinking, Jesus!" he cried, "Save me!" Jesus reached His hand out to Peter and lifted him up again. "Where did your faith go?" Jesus asked him. "If you had trusted Me, you wouldn't have fallen. Why do you doubt?" Then Jesus and Peter walked back together toward the boat. The other disciples had been watching the whole thing. "You really are the Son of God!" they said. They bowed down at Jesus' feet and worshiped Him.

Let the Children Come to Me
Mark 10:13-16

Many parents brought their children to Jesus hoping He would bless them. The children crowded around Jesus, but Jesus' disciples told them to stop. "Step back," they instructed the children. Jesus doesn't want to be bothered."

However, Jesus said, "Let the children come to Me! Don't stop them. These children belong to the kingdom of God. None of you can enter God's kingdom unless you accept it the way a child does. Learn from them!"

Then Jesus opened His arms and the little children ran giggling and smiling, wrapping their arms around Jesus' neck. Jesus placed His hands on them and blessed each one.

Following Jesus
Mark 10:23-31

Jesus said to His disciples, "It is easier for a camel to go through the eye of a needle than it is for a rich person to get into God's kingdom." The disciples were amazed. "But how can anyone ever be saved?" they cried. Jesus replied, "With people, this is impossible, but not with God. All things are possible with God."

Peter said, "We left everything to follow you, Jesus!"

"Anyone who gives up his home or his family or the things he owns for Me will be rewarded. You may be mistreated and persecuted because of Me, but in the world to come you will receive one hundred times as much as you gave up for Me! Many who are last here on earth will be first in heaven and many who are first now will later be last."

The Good Shepherd
John 10:11-18

Jesus said, "I am the good shepherd, and you are My flock. The shepherd will give up His life for His sheep. Hired workers don't own the sheep, so they do not care about them. When a wolf comes, they run off and leave the sheep to be taken and eaten. But, each little sheep is important to Me. If one is lost, I will search high and low until that

sheep is found! I love My sheep, and they love Me, just as the Father loves Me, and I love the Father. I bring all My sheep together into one flock and watch over them. I will gladly give up My life for My sheep. No one takes My life from Me—I give it up willingly! I have the power to give up My life and the power to receive it back again, just as My Father commanded Me to do."

The Death of Lazarus
John 11:1-16

When Jesus was in Jerusalem He often visited Mary and Martha and their brother, Lazarus, who lived close by in Bethany. They were some of Jesus' good friends. One day Lazarus got very sick. So Mary and Martha sent a message and told Jesus to come. Jesus got the news, but although he loved Mary, Martha, and Lazarus, He didn't go right away. He knew what God wanted Him to do.

Two days later, Jesus told His disciples to come with Him to see Lazarus. "But he lives in Judea," they answered, "why do You want to go? Only a few days ago the Jewish leaders in Judea were trying to kill You."

Jesus answered, "Our friend, Lazarus, is asleep. I want to wake him up."

"If he sleeps he'll get better, won't he?" His disciples asked. But they didn't understand what Jesus meant. "No, Lazarus is dead," He explained." But, I'm glad I wasn't there when he died, because now you will have a good reason to put your faith in Me. Let's go, and I'll show you."

Jesus Brings Lazarus to Life
John 11:17-44

When Martha saw that Jesus was coming, she ran out to meet Him. Jesus said, "I am the one who can raise the dead! Anyone who puts their faith in Me will live, even after death. Do you believe this, Martha?" "Yes, Lord!" she replied. "I know that You are the Son of God."

Then Mary came out. She went to Jesus and kneeled down in front of Him. "Lord, our brother is dead. If You had come sooner, I know he would've lived." Jesus was moved and started to weep. He walked over to Lazarus' tomb. "Roll the stone away," He told them. But Martha said, "Lord,

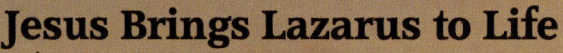

he's been dead for four days. There will be a bad smell." However, they rolled the stone away. Jesus looked up and prayed, "Father, I know You always answer My prayer. Let these people understand that You have sent Me." Then Jesus said, "Lazarus, come out!"

Lazarus came out of the tomb wrapped in burial cloth from head to toe. Jesus told Lazarus' family to take the grave cloths off him and let him go.

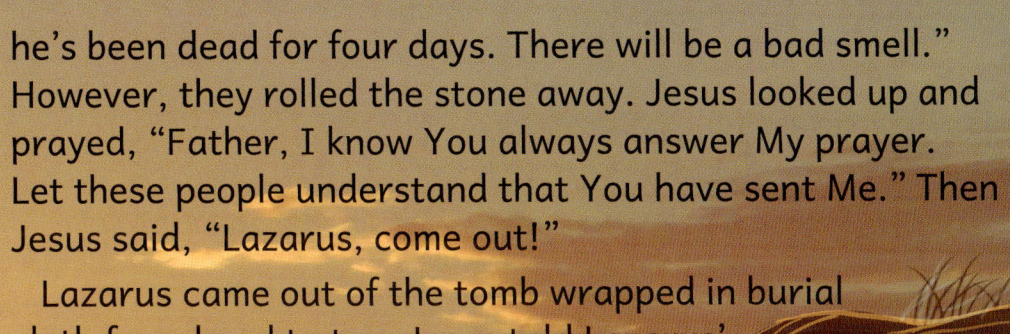

Who Gave the Most?
Mark 12:41-44

Jesus was sitting in the temple near the offering box. He was watching people put in their money gifts to God. The rich people put in handfuls of money. The coins clinked and

clanked as they fell into the box. Then, a poor widow went up to the box. She put in two coins that were worth about two pennies.

Jesus told His disciples to gather around. Then He said, "This poor widow has put in more than all the others." The disciples shook their heads and said, "She only put in two small coins!"

Jesus nodded. Then He said, "You see, the many coins of the rich do not mean much. They are like loose change in their pockets. But the few coins of the poor are as valuable as gold. This widow gave away everything she had to live on."

The Good Samaritan
Luke 10:29-37

One day, an expert of the law wanted to test Jesus. "What must I do to get eternal life?" he asked Jesus. "You shall love the Lord your God with all your heart, and your soul, and your mind," answered Jesus. "And you shall love your neighbor as yourself." Trying to justify himself, the teacher asked, "Who is my neighbor?" Jesus looked at him and said, "A man was traveling along a deserted road. Robbers came by and attacked him. They stole everything he had and left him lying in a pitiful heap by the roadside. Then they ran off. A priest was traveling down the road and came upon the man. He crossed over to the other side and kept on walking. Next, a temple worker came upon the man. He also crossed to the other side of the road and kept on walking. Finally, a Samaritan came by. When he saw the man, he stopped to help him. He treated his wounds with oil and wine and put him on his donkey. Then he took him to an inn and told the innkeeper, 'Please care for the man, and I will pay you however much it costs.'"

"Now," Jesus continued, "which of these three men would you say acted as a neighbor?"

The man who had asked the question said, "The one who showed pity."

Jesus answered, "Yes! Now go and do the same."

A Rich Fool
Luke 12:13-21

A young man in the crowd stood up and called to Jesus, "Teacher, tell my brother to be fair and give my share of what our father has left us!"

Jesus answered, "If I did that, it would not help you. What you own will not make your life any better than it is. Then Jesus continued, "There was a farmer who produced a harvest so big that he had to build several new barns

just to hold the grain. But God said to him, 'You fool! This night you'll die. What good is all your wealth then?' This is how it will be with anyone who stores up riches for himself but is not rich toward God."

Then Jesus said to the disciples, "Don't worry about your life, what you need to eat, drink, or wear—for your father in heaven will take care of you and give you everything you need."

The Lost Sheep and the Lost Coin
Luke 15:1-10

One day, when many tax collectors and other outcasts came to listen to Jesus, the Pharisees and the teachers of the Law started grumbling, "This man welcomes sinners and even eats with them!"

When Jesus heard them say these things, He turned and faced them.

"Imagine," Jesus said, "that you are a shepherd, and you have lost one of your sheep. Wouldn't you leave the ninety-nine others behind and find the lost one? When you find the sheep, you will be so glad that you will carry it home on your shoulders. Then you will say to your friends, 'Let's celebrate! I've found the one that was lost.'" Jesus continued, "There is more rejoicing in heaven over one sinner that turns to God than over ninety-nine good people who do not need to. What about a woman who loses one of her ten silver coins? Won't she light a lamp, sweep the floor, and look carefully until she has found it? My Father in heaven will celebrate when one of these sinners, who sit with Me now, turns to Him."

The Loving Father
Luke 15:11-19

Jesus told another story: "A man had two sons. He loved them both and wanted to see them do well. One day, the younger brother came to his father and said, 'Father, please give me my share.' Shortly after, he took off and traveled to a faraway country. There he spent all his money on wild living, and before he knew it, he reached into his pocket, and there was no money left. Desperate for money, he took a job working for a pig farmer. His clothes turned ragged and dirty. His stomach was always growling with hunger, and he would've been happy to eat the slop from the trough of the pigs. At last, he came to his senses. He thought, 'This is foolish! My father treats his servants better than this! I will go to him and ask his forgiveness. Perhaps he will accept me, and I will offer to work for him.' So the son started on the long journey home again, back to his father's house."

Forgiven
Luke 15:20-32

Jesus continued telling the story: "While the younger son was still far from home, his father spotted him on the road and his heart ached for his son. He ran out to meet him and showered him with hugs and kisses. He called to his servants, 'Bring out our finest clothes! Prepare a big feast! Put a shiny ring on my son's finger! He was lost, and now he is found!' Meanwhile the older son was out in the field working. He ran back to the house to see what had happened. 'What's going on?' he asked a servant. 'Your brother is back!' the servant replied. The older brother became angry. He ran to his father and said, 'I have been working like a slave for you. I have obeyed you. I have always done everything you asked me to. But my brother runs away, spends all your money on foolish things and disobeys you. Now why are you treating him like a prince?' His father answered, 'Son, all I have is yours. You always did right and obeyed me. You were never lost, but your brother was lost. Be happy and celebrate with me because he was like dead and now he is alive!'"

God Shows Mercy
Luke 18:9-14

One day, Jesus noticed some people who were arrogant and proud and looked down on everybody else, so He told a story: "Two men went into the temple to pray. One was a Pharisee and the other was a tax collector. The Pharisee prayed, 'Thank you God that I'm not like robbers, murderers, or even as the tax collector there. I am not greedy or dishonest. I am faithful in marriage, and I have always given part of my money to You.' However, the tax collector stayed in the far corner of the temple. He did not think he was good enough to even look up toward heaven. He hung his head and prayed, 'God, have mercy on me! I am such a sinner.' Whom do you think God was pleased with more?" Jesus asked. "Was it the man who bragged about how good he was or the man who admitted to his sins? Remember, if you hold yourself high above others, you will be put down, but if you are humble and admit your sins, you will be honored."

A Job Well Done
Luke 19:15-26

Jesus told this parable: "A man of noble birth was going on a journey to a distant country to be made king. But first, he summoned his three servants and gave them each the same amount of money. 'Put this money to work while I am away,' he said, then he left. Later, after he was made king, he returned home and summoned his servants again. 'Tell me what you have done with the money I gave you.' The first servant made ten times the amount and was put in charge of ten cities. The second servant made five times the amount and was put in charge of five cities. The last servant made no money. 'I was afraid of you, so I didn't want to risk losing your money.' The king was angry. 'You could at least have put it in the bank,' he said. Then he ordered that money to be given to the first servant. 'But he already

has plenty!' cried the king's officials. The king replied, 'Those who do what I say will be given more. Those who are fearful and do nothing will lose what they had been given.'"

The Greatest in Heaven
Matthew 18:1-5

One day, the disciples asked Jesus, "Who will be the greatest in God's kingdom?" Jesus looked around and saw a child peeking out from behind the people in the crowd. He called the child over and pulled him gently into His arms.

"I promise you this," said Jesus to the disciples. "If you don't change and become like this child, you will never get into the kingdom of heaven. A child accepts God with a pure and humble heart. If you do this, you will be the greatest in God's kingdom. When you welcome one of these children, you welcome Me."

I Am with You
Matthew 18:15-20

Jesus said, "If your friend sins against you, go and speak with that person. Do it just between the two of you. If that person listens, you have won back your friend. If that person refuses to listen, take along one or two others and speak with that person again. If the person still does not hear what you say, go to the whole church.

I promise you that whenever you pray with others and your hearts are one, My Father in heaven will answer your prayer. Whenever two or three of you come together in My name, I am there with you."

The Rich Young Man
Matthew 19:16-22

A rich man came to Jesus and asked, "Teacher, what good things must I do to get into heaven?" Jesus answered, "Only God is truly good. If you want to enter into heaven, obey God's words."

The man then asked, "Which words should I obey?" Jesus answered, "The commandments: Do not murder. Be faithful in marriage. Do not steal. Do not tell lies. Respect your parents. And love others as you do yourself!"

The man nodded. "Yes, Jesus. I have obeyed all of these rules," he said. "What else should I do?" Jesus replied, "If

you want to do more, go beyond simply obeying the rules. Sell the things you own, and give to those who do not have anything. Then, come and be My follower, and you will be on the right path."

When the young man heard this, he was sad, because he was very rich.

The Big Parade
Luke 19:28-38

Jesus was nearing Jerusalem. He sent two of His disciples ahead of Him. "Go into the next village," He instructed them. "You'll see a donkey tied to a pole. Untie the donkey, and bring it to Me. If anyone asks why you are taking it, tell them the Lord needs it."

The disciples went and found the donkey Jesus was talking about. As they began to untie it, the owner of the donkey snapped at them. "What do you think you're doing?" When they told him the Lord needed it, the man let them go. They brought the donkey to Jesus, and He climbed on its back. Then He rode down the Mount of Olives toward Jerusalem.

The people were waiting for Him down below. They laid their coats on the ground to make a path for Jesus and waved large palm branches. They said, "Blessed is the Lord our King! May there be peace and glory in the highest heaven!"

A New Command
John 13:31-35

Jesus told His disciples, "I will have to leave all of you soon. You will look for Me, but I won't be there. God is going to bring glory to His Son! My time has come to go and be with My Father. I will leave you with a new command. My command is that you love each other just as I have loved you. If you do as I say, then the world will know that you are truly My followers."

The Leaders Shall Serve
Luke 22:14, 24-30

Jesus and His disciples sat down to eat the Passover meal. While they were eating, one of them asked, "Who is the greatest among God's people?" All the disciples had a different opinion, so they began to argue.

Jesus told them, "Some of you may think a ruler is the greatest because he orders people around. But don't be like that. The greatest person is the one who serves others. I have been a servant to you"

"Soon, I will be gone. If you continue to serve, you will rule with Me in My kingdom. Each of you will have a throne, and you will eat and drink at My table."

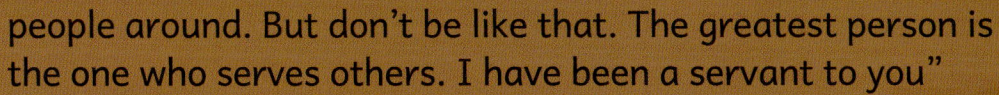

The Lord's Supper
Mark 14:18-24

Jesus told His disciples, "One of you eating with Me is going to betray Me." The disciples hung their heads.

They felt sad. "Surely You don't mean me?" each of them asked Jesus. "I would never do a thing like that," each of them said. Jesus told them, "One of you twelve will turn your back on Me. I will die and go to the Father. It will be terrible for the man who betrays Me. He will wish he had never been born." Jesus picked up the loaf of bread from the table. He gave thanks and broke the bread in two. "Take this bread and eat it," He told them. "It is My body broken for you." Then Jesus took the cup of wine, gave thanks, and passed it around. "Take this wine and drink it. It is My blood poured out for many. My blood seals the new covenant." So the disciples ate and drank. Jesus told them, "I will give up my body for you so that your sins may be forgiven."

Peter Will Deny Jesus
Mark 14:26-31

When the disciples had finished their meal, they sang a hymn and left the place. They went to the Mount of Olives. While they were there, Jesus told them, "I will die, and each one of you will turn your back on Me. You will be scattered and lost like sheep, but this won't be the end. I will come back and lead you again."

Peter said, "Lord, even if the others turn their backs on You, I never will."

However, Jesus knew the truth. He said, "You will reject Me this very night. Before the rooster crows, three times you will say that you don't know Me."

Peter didn't believe Him. "No, I will never do that," he replied. All the other disciples said the same thing.

A Home in Heaven
John 14:1-7

The disciples felt sad and Jesus could see it in their faces, so He told them, "Don't worry! Have faith in God, and have faith in Me. It's true that I cannot stay with you. But there are many rooms in God's house. I am going ahead of you to prepare a place where we can be together. I wouldn't tell you this if it weren't true."

"Lord," the disciple Thomas replied, "we don't know where You're going. How can we follow You if we don't know the way?"

Jesus told him, "I am the way, the truth, and the life! The only way to My Father is through Me."

The Disciples Fall Asleep
Mark 14:33-42

Jesus felt sad and troubled. He knew He was going to die soon. "Will you stay awake and pray with Me?" He asked His disciples. He walked a few steps away and knelt in the grass, "Abba, Father! You can do all things. Take this cup of suffering away from Me. But do what You want, not what I want."

Jesus went back to His disciples. They had all fallen asleep. He said to Peter, "Can't you stay awake with Me for one hour?" But they couldn't keep their eyes open. They just mumbled and fell asleep again after Jesus left to pray.

One last time, He went back to the

disciples. "Wake up! It's time for Me to be taken away from you. The one who has betrayed Me is already coming this way into the garden."

Betrayed With a Kiss
John 18:2-8; Matthew 26:48-49

Judas Iscariot, one of the disciples, had told the Roman soldiers where they could find Jesus. "He will be in the garden with the other disciples, and you will know who Jesus is because I'll give Him a kiss on the cheek." The plan was settled. They lit their torches and carried their

weapons following Judas to the garden of Gethsemane.

Jesus saw them coming. "Who are you looking for?" He asked them.

"We've come to arrest Jesus," they answered.

"I am He," He said. When Jesus said this, the soldiers drew back and fell to the ground. So Jesus asked them again, "Who are you looking for?"

"We've come for Jesus," they answered.

"I am the one you want, so if you are seeking Me, let My disciples go," Jesus said. Then Judas walked up to Jesus and kissed Him on the cheek. The soldiers grabbed Jesus and arrested Him.

Pilate Tries to Free Jesus
John 18:28-40

Jesus was first taken to the chief priest's house, where He was charged with blasphemy because He said He was the Son of God. Then He was taken to the palace of the Roman governor, Pilate, to be tried. There was a large crowd gathered outside Pilate's palace, so he came out and asked what the problem was. When Pilate heard it was a charge of blasphemy he said, "Since it is about your religion, why don't you punish Him?"

The people cried back, "It's against the law for us to crucify Him. We need you to do it! He also calls Himself a king." So Pilate went back inside and asked Jesus. "Are You the King of the Jews? The people are saying that You call Yourself a king," Pilate said. "My kingdom does not belong to this world," Jesus replied. "If it did, My servants would have fought to keep Me from being given over to the Jewish leaders." "So," Pilate said, "You admit to being a king!"

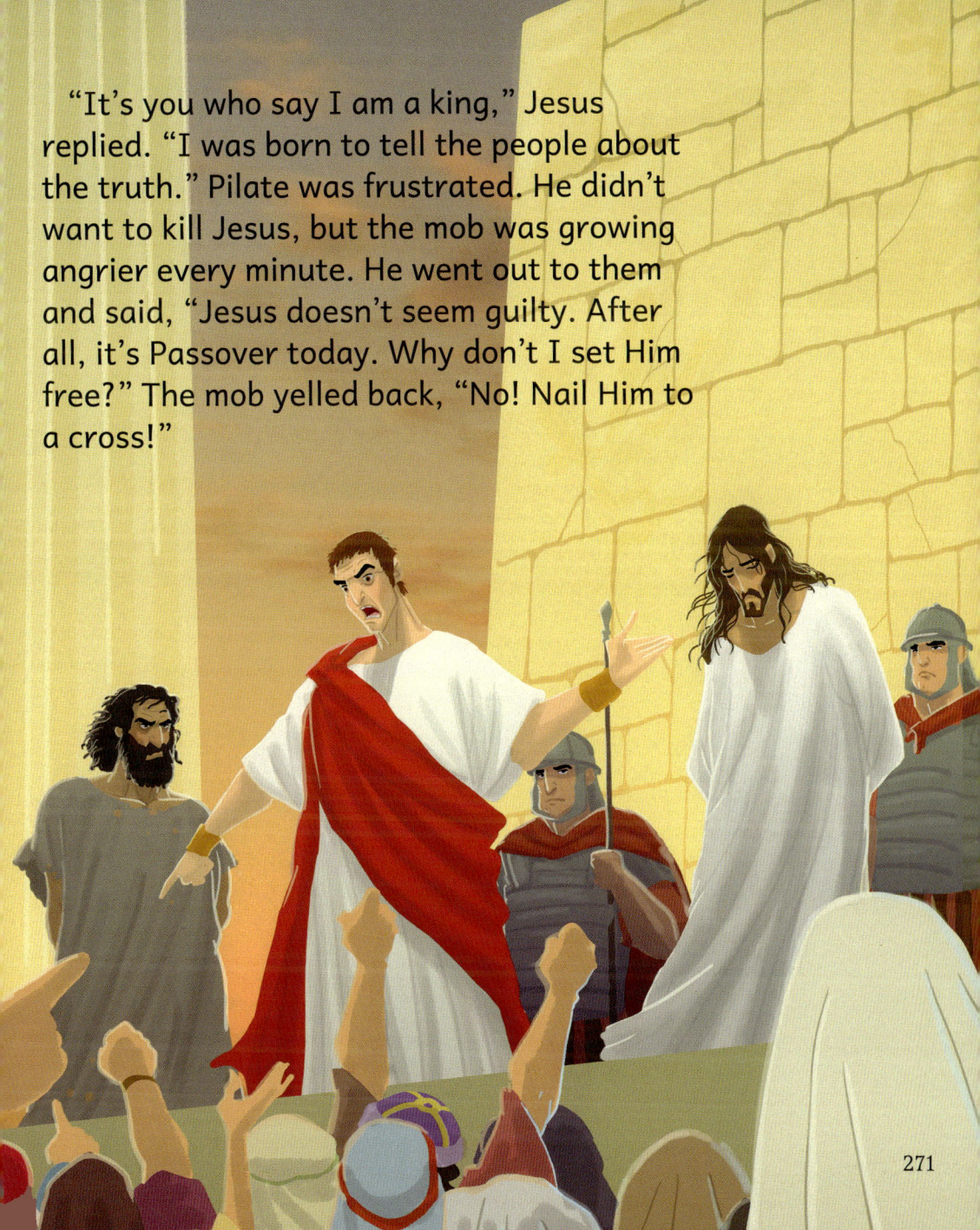

"It's you who say I am a king," Jesus replied. "I was born to tell the people about the truth." Pilate was frustrated. He didn't want to kill Jesus, but the mob was growing angrier every minute. He went out to them and said, "Jesus doesn't seem guilty. After all, it's Passover today. Why don't I set Him free?" The mob yelled back, "No! Nail Him to a cross!"

Jesus Is Sentenced to Death
John 19:1-16

Pilate tried to calm the mob, but the people kept shouting because the priests urged them to. "Tie Jesus up, and we'll beat Him," Pilate told his soldiers. "That should satisfy the people." So the soldiers beat Jesus and put a crown of thorns on His head, but the people were not satisfied. "Crucify Him! Crucify Him!" they chanted.

Pilate went over to Jesus. "Where do You come from?" he asked. But Jesus was silent. "Why don't You answer me? Don't You know I have the power to free You?"

Jesus lifted His wearied head and replied, "Only God has the power to free Me. Without His permission, you couldn't do anything at all to Me."

Pilate asked the mob again, "So, you really want me to kill your king?"

"He's not our king," the people yelled back. "Only the emperor is king." Pilate finally gave in and handed Jesus over to be killed.

Jesus Is Nailed to a Cross
Luke 23:32-38

They nailed Jesus to a cross. There was a sign above His head that read, "The King of the Jews." The soldiers crucified two criminals alongside Jesus, while the people watched from down below. Some of them made fun of Jesus and called Him names. "Why can't You save

Yourself?" the soldiers taunted Him. "We thought You were the Lord!" They also gambled for His clothes.

While Jesus was on the cross, He prayed, "Forgive these people, Father! They don't know what they're doing."

Jesus Dies
Luke 23:39-44; John 19:28-30

One of the criminals who was also being crucified shouted insults to Jesus: "Aren't You the Lord? Save Yourself and save us!"

The other criminal told him, "Don't You fear God? We are punished for doing wrong, but Jesus is truly innocent." Then he said to Jesus, "Remember me when You come to Your kingdom."

Jesus replied, "I promise that today you will be with Me in Paradise." The sun stopped shining and the sky turned dark. Jesus knew His time was almost done. "I'm thirsty!" He said. So someone soaked a sponge with vinegar, tied it to a long plant stem, and lifted it to Jesus' mouth. He said, "It is finished!" and He bowed His head and died.

The Earth Trembles
Matthew 27:51-54

The moment Jesus died, the heavy curtain in Jerusalem's temple was torn in two, from top to bottom, the earth shook, rocks split apart and graves opened. The bodies of many Godly men and women who had died were raised from the dead. (Later, after Jesus rose to life again, they would walk into Jerusalem and appear to many people.) Many of the soldiers and leaders of Israel were scared when all these things happened.

They thought to themselves, "Jesus must have truly been the Son of God!"

Jesus Is Buried
John 19:31-42

The next day was the Sabbath. The people wanted the bodies to be taken down from the crosses before this special day.

The soldiers took down Jesus' body and two of Jesus' secret followers, named Joseph of Arimathea and Nicodemus, got permission from Pilate to bury Jesus. They had bought spiced ointment, a mixture of myrrh and aloe, and white linen to wrap His body. Then they put Him in a tomb that had been cut out in the rocks. They rolled a heavy stone over the entrance and left.

Jesus Has Risen
Matthew 28:1-10

Mary Magdalene went to visit Jesus' tomb with the other Mary. An earthquake rumbled and shook the ground. The soldiers, who were guarding Jesus' tomb, were so frightened that they fainted. An angel of the Lord came down from heaven and rolled the heavy round stone away from the tomb. His clothes were bright white, and his face was shining. "Don't be afraid," the angel told the women. "I know you've come to see Jesus, but He isn't here. God has raised Him to life!"

The women were speechless. They started running back to town—full of joy and excitement. They couldn't wait to tell the disciples what the angel had said! While they were on their way, Jesus suddenly met them. The women came up to Jesus, took hold of His feet, and worshiped Him. "Don't be afraid," He said with a smile, "Go and tell My disciples that I will meet them in Galilee."

The Empty Tomb
John 20:2-10

Mary Magdalene found Simon Peter and said, "The tomb is empty! Jesus is no longer there!" Peter had to see it with his own eyes. He immediately got up and ran toward the tomb. Another disciple went with him and got there before Peter. He didn't go inside, so Peter went in first. Jesus wasn't there! He saw the linen that had been wrapped around Jesus' body. The cloth that had covered Jesus' head lay nicely folded by itself. The other disciple came inside, too. He saw and believed. The two of them went back to tell the other disciples.

Jesus Returns to God
Acts 1:3-11

Jesus stayed with His disciples for forty days after He had risen from the grave. He spoke of the Kingdom of God and said, "John baptized you with water, but in a few days, you will be baptized with the Holy Spirit."

The disciples had many questions, but Jesus said, "Do not worry, the Holy Spirit will come to you and you will receive power. You will be My witnesses—in Jerusalem, in all of Judea, in Samaria, and in every part of the world." After He said this, Jesus rose up in the sky to heaven as they watched.

His disciples stood staring up at the sky where Jesus had disappeared into the clouds when two strangers in white stood beside them and asked, "Why do you stand here? You saw Jesus go up into heaven, but He will return in the same way you saw Him leave."

Paul

As he neared Damascus on his journey, suddenly a light from heaven flashed around him. He fell to the ground and heard a voice say to him, "Saul, Saul, why do you persecute me?" "Who are you, Lord?" Saul asked. "I am Jesus, whom you are persecuting," he replied. "Now get up and go into the city, and you will be told what you must do."
Acts 9:3-6

- Mentioned in: Acts, Romans, 1 Corinthians, 2 Corinthians, Galatians, Ephesians, Philippians, Colossians, 1 Thessalonians, 1 Timothy, 2 Timothy, Titus, Philemon, 2 Peter, Titus, Philemon, 2 Peter (all of which he wrote)
- Meaning of name: "Small or humble" --his Hebrew birth name was Saul ("Asked for") but God changed his name on the road to Damascus
- Lived in: Tarsus (modern day Turkey), studied in Jerusalem, later traveled to many parts of the Roman Empire
- Married to: None (Paul never married)
- Father of: None, but many spiritual children (people who followed Jesus because of Paul's ministry)

Milestones:

Paul converted to Christianity after meeting Jesus on the road to Damascus. This made him believe in Jesus and His message, so he immediately went out to spread the Good News. Paul was a small man, but he had a great heart and a sharp mind. He knew that God's Word needed to be spread in a special way, and so, using his intelligence and heart, he created a ministry that brought Jesus' Word all across the ancient World.

Questions:

One moment Paul was on his way to persecute those who believed in Jesus, but then, after seeing Jesus, he turned around and preached the Gospel. He was brave in deciding to change, even though it was not the easiest choice. Have you ever experienced a change in your life? Do you have a change coming up like moving to a new house or a new school? How can you lean on Jesus and be brave?

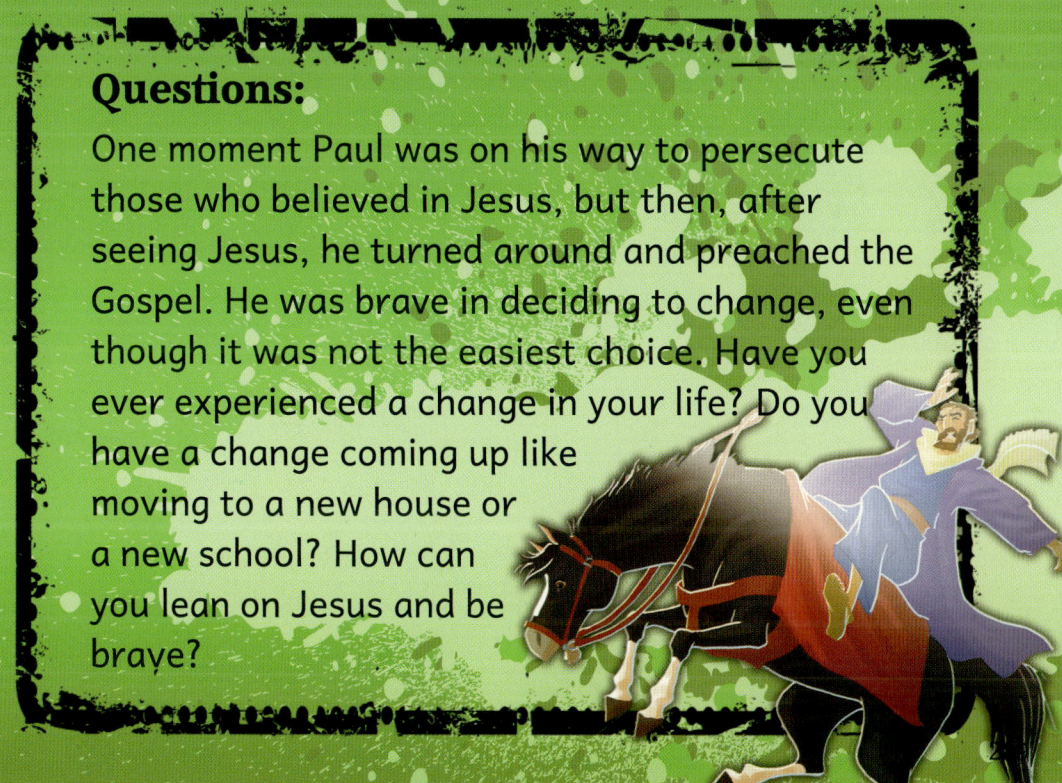

Saul on the Road to Damascus
Acts 9:1-19

Saul was a strong believer in the Jewish ways of following God's laws. He wanted to round up all Jesus' followers and throw them in jail. One day, as he was nearing Damascus to find Christians, a light shone and burned in his eyes. The light got brighter until Saul could not see anything! He fell to the ground and heard a voice call to him, "Saul, why are you fighting against me?" Saul asked, "Who are You?" The voice replied, "I am Jesus whom you are persecuting! Get up and go to Damascus. I will tell you what to do when you get there." Saul had been blinded by the Lord's light, so the men who were with him led him by the hand into Damascus.

Three days later, God sent a disciple named Ananias to Saul. Ananias laid his hands on Saul's head and said, "Saul, Jesus has sent me so that you may get your sight back and be filled with the Holy Spirit." Saul opened his eyes. He could see again! Saul was baptized and stayed for several days with the followers of Jesus in Damascus.

Paul and Silas in Jail
Acts 16:16-24

After Saul met Jesus, he began to spread the good news about Him everywhere, even in other countries. He changed his name to Paul. Even though he was mistreated, Paul continued to do the Lord's work.

One day, in the city of Philippi, he and his companion, Silas, met a slave girl who had an evil spirit inside her. It gave her the ability to tell fortunes. Her owners made a lot of money from her being able to do this. She followed

behind Paul and Silas shouting, "These men are servants of the Most High God, and they have come to tell you how to be saved." She did this for many days, until Paul became so upset that he turned around and said to the spirit, "In the name of Jesus Christ, I order you to come out of her!" The spirit came out at once and the girl calmed down, but her owners were infuriated. She had lost her ability to tell fortunes, and they could no longer make money off of her. They brought Paul and Silas before the city officials and said, "These Jews are making trouble in our city!" The crowd around them joined in the attack against them, so the city officials arrested Paul and Silas. They beat them, threw them into jail, and shackled their feet so they couldn't move.

Singing in Jail
Acts 16:25-36

About midnight in the jail, Paul and Silas were singing songs of worship, and the prisoners were listening to them. Suddenly, the ground began to shake, and the chains that bound them rattled furiously. God was sending an earthquake! The chains burst and broke, and the cell doors opened! The jailor was frightened. He thought all the prisoners would escape and he would be in big trouble. In his panic, he reached for his sword to kill himself, but Paul cried out, "Stop! We have not run away. There is no need to harm yourself!" The jailor was full of gratitude. He bent down at the feet of Paul and said, "You are a good man. You have shown me mercy. What must I do to be saved?" Paul answered, "Believe in the Lord Jesus and you will be saved!" The jailor took Paul and Silas to his house, washed their wounds, and gave them a meal. Then Paul baptized the jailor and his whole family. The next morning the city officials released them.

A Mob Turns Against Paul
Acts 21:27-35

Paul returned to Jerusalem to meet with his friends and some of the church elders. They were glad he had come. However, some people who had met him abroad recognized Paul in the temple and grabbed him, yelling, "This is the man who teaches things that are against the Law of Moses!" They dragged Paul out of the temple, and immediately the gates were closed behind him. As they were trying to

kill Paul, the Roman army commander heard the uproar and sent some soldiers to rescue him and yelled, "What has this man done?" Everybody began to shout at once. "He's a liar!" one said. "He's a friend of our enemies!" said another. Others in the crowd began to yell different things. The voices turned into a great big clamor of noise. The army commander could not make out what any of them were saying. He decided he must do something, so he had Paul arrested to satisfy the angry crowd.

Paul Speaks Before the Governor
Acts 24:24-27; 25:8-12

After some time, Paul was transferred to Caesarea. A man named Felix was serving as governor in Caesarea. Felix was one of those who would visit Paul while he was in jail. He listened as Paul talked about believing in Jesus, but Felix became afraid when Paul talked about things like living right, having self-control, and God judging the world. He was hoping Paul would offer him money in exchange for his freedom, but Paul never bribed him. Two years later, a man named Festus took the place of Felix as governor of Caesarea. One day, Festus came to Paul and asked him if he was ready to be judged and charged for his crimes. Paul answered, "I have not done anything wrong. If I had done something deserving death, I would accept it. But I will go anyway and be judged by the Emperor of Rome who has the highest authority."

A Stormy Voyage
Acts 27

Paul boarded the ship to Rome with some other prisoners and the captain and crew. They sailed along smoothly until they came to a harbor called Safe Harbors. Paul suggested to the captain that they stay there until the winter had passed. He knew there might be dangerous storms at sea this time of year. But the captain insisted they sail on. Soon they were hit by a mighty storm and driven far off course. The crew wrapped rope around the ship to hold it together, for the waves pounded against it. The storm continued for many days until all their hope of being saved was gone. Then Paul told the people, "Don't be afraid! An angel from God told me last night that we will all be rescued, but we must run aground onto an island."

The captain of the ship spotted a cove of sand off in the distance. Before they could reach the cove, the crashing waves had grown so fierce that they wrecked the ship. The captain ordered everybody to jump overboard and swim toward the cove. Those who couldn't swim held on to planks from the broken ship.

Rome at Last
Acts 28

Paul and the others swam with all their might against the angry sea. Finally, they reached the sandy cove and collapsed on the shore. They had come to an island called Malta. The islanders of Malta welcomed the shipwrecked people. They built a fire to help them get warm. Paul was gathering some wood when suddenly a snake came out and bit him on the finger. The islanders cried out, "That's a poisonous snake. You will die!" But Paul just shook the snake off, and he didn't die. The islanders were stunned. They were certain Paul was a god. Who else could survive a poisonous snakebite? Paul rejected their claims. Instead, he prayed for the sick, and they were healed.

   Once spring arrived and the sea was calm again, Paul and the others boarded another ship and finally arrived in Rome. Paul was allowed to stay in a rented house while he waited for the Emperor to call him into court to be judged. Many people in Rome had heard about Paul. He kept his door wide open and invited strangers and friends alike to come and talk about Jesus with him. His house became a popular meeting place for all the followers of Jesus. Paul spoke very boldly about Christ, and no one stopped him.